The Cape MALAY COOKBOOK

STRUIK PUBLISHERS

The Cape MALAY
COOKBOOK

Faldela Williams

Photography by Cornel de Kock

Struik Lifestyle
(an imprint of Random House Struik (Pty) Ltd)
Company Reg. No. 1966/003153/07
Wembley Square, Solan Road, Gardens, Cape Town 8001
PO Box 1144, Cape Town, 8000, South Africa

First published in 1993 in softcover by Struik Publishers
Reprinted 13 times (1995–2008)
Reprinted in 2010 (twice), 2012 by Struik Lifestyle

Copyright © in published edition:
Random House Struik (Pty) Ltd 1993, 2010
Copyright © in text: Faldela Williams 1993, 2010
Copyright © in photographs:
Random House Struik (Pty) Ltd 1993, 2010

Publisher: Linda de Villiers
Designer: Joan Sutton
Editors: Pat Barton and Marje Hemp
Illustrator: Felicity Harris
Typesetting: Unifoto (Pty) Ltd
Reproduction: Hirt & Carter Cape (Pty) Ltd
Printing and binding: Tien Wah Press (Pte) Ltd, Singapore

ISBN 978-1-86825-560-3

*To my husband, Ebrahim, who has always been my
greatest critic as far as my food is concerned, and my
children for their love and appreciation.*

Acknowledgements

Writing this book, as well as finding authentic props and preparing food for the photography,
has been a great challenge and I would like to thank my family and friends for their support
and encouragement. In particular I wish to thank the following for making this book a
reality:
• My mother, Mrs Galiema Adams, and my sister, Fawzia; Aunty Haya Jonas, Aunty Gawa
Amos, Aunty Bieba Mohammed and Mrs Shariefa Najaar for assisting me with traditional
Malay recipes.
• My grandmother, Mrs Jogera Adams, Aunty Haya Jonas, Gawie Mohammed,
Aunty Radiefa Nordien, Fawzia van der Westhuizen, Alieja Eksteen, Soraya Valley,
Mrs Zubeida Manan, Tougeedah Bassadien and Mrs Wareldia da Costa for lending me their
special dishes, delicate chinaware, brassware, beautiful cut-glass containers and other props
for the photographs.
• Pat Barton, who spent many hours editing my manuscript to bring a semblance of order to
my collection of recipes, and Marje Hemp for giving me an opportunity of a life-time.
• Shelly Street, for styling the food for the photographs, and Lauren Tait and
Shahieda Majiet for assisting me with some of the cooking.

Contents

Foreword

This book by Faldela Williams on traditional 'Malay' cooking is an important contribution to the preservation of this country's culinary tradition. The author has managed, after considerable research and investigation, to bring together into a single volume the numerous recipes for the dishes which are so common in many of the Muslim homes in the Cape Peninsula today.

The importance of her effort lies not only in her giving recognition to the major contribution made by different peoples of Asian origin to South African cuisine, but also in her interesting pieces of social history that are found with some of the recipes.

I am positive that this book will find a ready market in this and other countries; especially for those people who see cooking as part of a cultural tradition and practise it as a culinary art.

Y. Da Costa
Lecturer, Faculty of Education
University of the Western Cape.

Author's Preface

My interest in cooking started when I was a young girl living in my grandmother's house in District Six. My grandmother was well known for her baking and the tasty dishes that she prepared with such care and attention not only for her large family, but also for the Muslim community to which we belonged. She spent much of her time in the kitchen preparing bredies, breyani, atjar and blatjang as well as koesisters, melktert, cakes and biscuits for religious feasts, engagements, weddings and funerals in our neighbourhood. As a ten year old, I was allowed to help decorate the biscuits and clean the vegetables. Later on, my Saturdays were spent frying koesisters because my grandmother was also a koesister vendor. At that stage, I also remember visiting my other grandmother, who allowed me to experiment with puddings, especially pineapple dessert (page 71), which was her favourite. Most of the time, I would go back to her home the next day and eat half of it myself.

In preparing the recipes for this book, I chose those that are practical and easy to make, and where necessary I have shortened complicated cooking methods to save time. When I began researching the more traditional recipes, however, I found great difficulty in obtaining the exact quantities for the ingredients, as most of the older Malay cooks estimate rather than measure the amounts required. Before including these recipes, I tested them at home. Much to my surprise, I found that they were a great favourite with my young family. These days Muslim cooks are more daring in trying out new recipes and I have included a few modern dishes, adapted to the Malay style, as well as microwave tips and freezer hints for the busy cook.

Bis'millah

Faldela Williams

Introduction

Cape Malay cooking has had considerable influence on South African culinary traditions and its virtues have been extolled by such writers and epicures as Laurens van der Post and Louis Leipoldt. Although it is predominantly Indonesian in origin, Malay cooking has been largely influenced by Indian cuisine hence the curries, rotis and samoosas. The baked puddings, tarts and biscuits show a strong Dutch influence, while the delicious fruit preserves are mainly French Huguenot in origin.

The name Cape Malay is perhaps something of a misnomer as it refers to followers of the Islamic faith, whose forefathers were brought to the Cape as slaves from the Indonesian island of Java, over 300 years ago. They were not associated with Malaysia in any way, except that they spoke Malay, a kind of universal language in that part of the world.

From its very beginning, South Africa has been a melting pot where East meets West. In the 17th Century, Malay cooks were very much sought after in the predominantly Dutch homes and soon learned how to prepare solid Dutch fare such as melktert, but added their own embellishment of grated nutmeg or cinnamon. They also used the exotic spices of the land of their birth to create such well-known dishes as bobotie, sosaties and pickled fish, which were almost always accompanied by chilli atjars, blatjangs and sambals. Many Malays were also expert fishermen, so that fish, especially snoek, and other seafoods became an important part of their diet, and the sound of the fish horn is still remembered by many Malays of an older generation. Sweetmeats, like syrupy koesisters and crunchy tameletjies, ever-popular delicacies were reserved for Sundays and feast days. Desserts were not all that common and most of the fruit found in abundance at the Cape was eaten fresh or it was preserved in a light sugar syrup.

Islamic Dietary Laws

Any food eaten by a Muslim should be Halaal or 'lawful', in other words religiously approved. Islam prescribes healthy, wholesome foods and like Judaism, forbids the eating of pork, blood and any animal or bird that has not been slaughtered in a humane way, usually with a swift stroke of a knife, so that it dies an almost painless death. The blood is always allowed to drain away thus giving the flesh better keeping qualities. Lamb is the most popular meat, followed by chicken and beef. Fish and seafoods are deemed Halaal according to the Holy Quran, which also forbids the drinking of alcohol.

Malay Etiquette

Before eating and afterwards, a Muslim is required to wash his hands and rinse his mouth. Then *Bis'millah* (In the name of Allah) is said by the host. Food should be eaten with the fingers of the right hand, although eating with a knife and fork is also becoming accepted these days. At social gatherings men and women may still eat apart, but normally the family enjoy their meal together in the evenings.

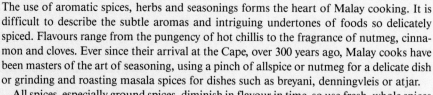

Spices, Herbs and Seasonings

The use of aromatic spices, herbs and seasonings forms the heart of Malay cooking. It is difficult to describe the subtle aromas and intriguing undertones of foods so delicately spiced. Flavours range from the pungency of hot chillis to the fragrance of nutmeg, cinnamon and cloves. Ever since their arrival at the Cape, over 300 years ago, Malay cooks have been masters of the art of seasoning, using a pinch of allspice or nutmeg for a delicate dish or grinding and roasting masala spices for dishes such as breyani, denningvleis or atjar.

All spices, especially ground spices, diminish in flavour in time, so use fresh, whole spices whenever possible and grind them only when you need them. Buy your spices from a recognized spice shop for the best results and store in airtight containers in a cool, dry place as they tend to lose their freshness if exposed too long to air, heat and moisture.

Allspice

This sun-dried berry of the West indian pimento tree seems to combine the flavours of nutmeg, cinnamon and cloves, hence its name. It is used in the preparation of many masalas and is therefore a popular spice in curries, soups and bredies. Ground allspice can also be used to flavour desserts, cakes and biscuits.

Aniseed

A seed similar in shape to that of jeera and barishap, but it is used mainly in confectionery because of its warm, sweet, pungent flavour similar to liquorice. Use sparingly, otherwise the flavour can be overpowering. Star aniseed, so called because of its star shape, is rarely used on its own but is ground and used in breyani masala and garam masala.

Barishap

The Malay name for fennel. Barishap seeds look very much like jeera but are less elongated and fatter. The seeds are aromatic with a warm, slightly bitter, aniseed flavour and are used in savoury dishes such as chevra and fish dishes. Ground barishap is very often used in breyani masala.

Bay leaf

The bay leaf comes from the sweet bay or true laurel tree. It is aromatic with a slightly bitter taste and is used in the preparation of pickled fish, sosaties and denningvleis. Use sparingly and always discard whole leaves before serving. For a more delicate flavour, some cooks prefer to use lemon leaves instead of bay leaves.

Borrie

Borrie, also called turmeric, is a deep yellow, ground spice obtained from the dried root of a plant related to ginger. It has a slightly bitter taste and care should be taken not to exceed the amount recommended in a recipe. Borrie is chiefly used in curries, pickled fish and sosaties and for colouring yellow rice.

Cardamom

Known as elachi in the Indian community. The dried seed pods are available in two varieties – green or white. It is best to buy cardamom seeds in small quantities and to use as needed, since they quickly lose their pungent aroma and distinctive flavour after they have been ground. The aromatic dark brown seeds are generally left whole or are lightly crushed for

curries, breyanis and other rice dishes. Ground cardamom is also used in the preparation of puddings, koesisters, biscuits and cakes.

Chilli

There are over 30 different varieties of chillis, some much sharper than others. Unripe or green chillis are jucier, with more flavour, while ripe red chillis are hotter. Pounded or liquidized chillis mixed with a little oil and salt can be stored in sealed containers in a refrigerator for easy use. Dried chillis should be torn into pieces and soaked in hot water for 10 minutes to soften. Chillis are a must for most curry dishes, chutneys and sambals, so experiment for the best results.

Chilli powder

Generally red in colour and made from dried red chillis. It is excellent for foods that need a bit of colour and gives an extra bite that makes quite a difference. Use instead of ground black pepper on chops and fish.

Cinnamon

The bark of a tropical tree which has a rich, strong, spicy aroma and a delicious, sweet flavour. In Malay cooking, stick cinnamon is added to curries, breyanis, vegetables, puddings and desserts. Ground cinnamon is also used in baking, melktert and confectionery.

Cloves

Cloves are the dried, unopened buds of yet another tree indigenous to Indonesia. They have a pronounced aroma and a strong, almost bitingly sharp, spicy taste. Cloves are used to flavour many savoury and sweet dishes, and the flavour blends well with other spices like cinnamon, allspice and nutmeg. Ground cloves are stronger than whole ones, so take care to use only a pinch or the flavour will be too overpowering.

Curry leaves

These are available fresh or dried. Fresh ones are mainly used for garnishing curry dishes while dried curry leaves are used in the preparation of leaf masalas and for adding extra flavour to savouries such as chevra.

Curry powder

This mixture of borrie, whole coriander, jeera, ginger, fenugreek, black peppercorns, chilli and mustard seeds is best when freshly ground. Many commercial preparations, including curry paste, are also available, but these do not have the flavour of fresh aromatic spices and tend to lend a sameness to everything in which they are used. Malay people mostly use masala in cooking and only use curry powder in sweet/sour curry dishes such as penang curry, sosaties, bobotie and pickled fish.

Dhunia

This is the name given to fresh coriander leaves which are used as a garnish in curry dishes or in the preparation of savouries such as samoosas. Pounded dhunia leaves are also an important ingredient for some chutneys. When crushed, dhunia leaves have an unmistakable pungent smell. They can also be chopped and used like parsley.

Garlic

A popular herb and a member of the onion family which is often used fresh in combination with fresh root ginger, although in fish dishes only garlic is used. Garlic minced or liquidized with a little oil and salt will last well in the refrigerator, is always ready to use and saves time.

Ginger

Ginger, like nearly all spices, contains a volatile oil that gives it its distinctive flavour which is aromatic, biting and slightly sweet. Fresh ginger is indispensible for making curries and breyanis and mixed with garlic makes an excellent meat tenderizer. Dried whole ginger is more fibrous and less aromatic than fresh, but is more pungent. It can be powdered easily and retains its spicy flavour for a long time. Ground ginger is used in flavouring koesisters, konfyts, puddings and cakes.

Jeera

The Malay and Indian term for cumin, a caraway-shaped seed that looks like fennel but is slightly more bitter. When the seeds are ground, the powder has a distinctive green colour. Jeera is an important ingredient for making various masalas, so is always used in curries and breyanis.

Koljander

Also known as coriander, a seed which tastes sweet and aromatic and should be roasted before being ground to bring out a more curry-like flavour. Koljander seeds crushed together with jeera are widely used in curries and other meat dishes.

Masala

Masala is a fragrant blend of spices used in curries, breyanis, atjars and many other savoury dishes. There are many different varieties of masala including wet and dry masala. There are special masalas for fish (with mustard seeds), vegetables, atjars, chutneys, breyanis and rice dishes. Buy freshly ground masala from a spice shop or make your own as needed and use the spices best suited to the particular dish you are preparing. You can grind your spices with a simple pestle and mortar, a blender or a food processor.

Atjar masala: A special mixture of spices including mustard seed, chilli powder, borrie, ground methi and salt. Oil is added to make a thick paste.

Breyani masala: Made with whole jeera seeds, koljander, barishap, bay leaves, cardamom, cinnamon and star aniseed. Roast and grind before using.

Garam masala: A fragrant, rather than hot, mixture of spices which is sometimes added with other spices at the frying stage, but is more generally added during the last few minutes of cooking or sprinkled over the food just before it is served.

Green masala: Contains pounded fresh ginger, garlic, green chilli and dhunia leaves.

Leaf masala: There are many varieties including red leaf masala, which has more ground chilli powder and is therefore hotter. Use for making meat curry. Yellow masala is similar to red leaf masala except that it has less chilli powder. Use for a milder curry.

Methi

Also known as fenugreek. Mostly only the hard lentil-type seed is used. Ground with other spices, it is used to make curry powder or methi masala which is used to flavour some rice and vegetable dishes. This spice has an astringent aroma and should be used sparingly.

Mint

When chopped, this clean-tasting herb blends well with savoury fillings for samoosas. Mint is very easy to grow and no garden, no matter how small, need be without this most useful herb. Mint leaves are used to great advantage for garnishing fresh fruit salads and punch.

Mustard seed

A dark reddish-brown seed, slightly bigger than a poppy seed. Seafood dishes, atjars and pickles are greatly enhanced when flavoured with mustard seeds. Add whole mustard seeds to atjar masala for a more pungent flavour.

Naartjie peel

This is one of the cheapest and most rewarding flavouring agents for puddings, desserts and vegetables and it is a great pity that so few people take the trouble to experiment with it nowadays. The peel is left out to dry in the sun, then ground into a powder and stored in an airtight jar for later use. It blends well with cardamom and cinnamon.

Nutmeg

A spice which comes from the same tree as mace. The seed of the fruit is the nutmeg and the dried, reddish skin that covers the nutmeg is mace. Grated or ground nutmeg is frequently used as a garnish for boiled vegetables, and as a flavouring in bredies and confectionery.

Rosewater

A fragrant essence distilled from rose petals. Traditionally, Malay cooks never used any essences, only rosewater was used to flavour boeber, a rich milky drink, and puddings. Nowadays rosewater is also used in the making of Turkish Delight. It is also an essential ingredient in rose syrup which is used to flavour milkshakes and falooda jelly.

Saffron

Saffron is by far the rarest and most expensive spice in the world. The name is derived from the Arabic word *Za'faran* meaning yellow. The dark, reddish-orange stamens of the wild crocus are used mainly for colouring and flavouring rice dishes and puddings. It is one of the most wonderful spices to use in breyani. To use, first infuse in hot water or add directly to the meat marinade when making breyani.

Tamarind

This dark brown fruit of a tropical tree tastes very much like an apricot/date mixture. Its sweet/sour flavour makes it an excellent ingredient in sosaties and denningvleis. Children love to suck on the fresh fruit.

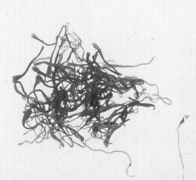

Snacks and Soups

SAMOOSAS

Samoosas are very time consuming to make, but are well worth the effort. If you are in a hurry use thin sheets of phyllo pastry or springroll wrappers instead of *pur*. I like to deep-fry strips of leftover *pur* to make a crunchy snack called *paaper*.

Pur *(pastry)*
750 ml cake flour
pinch borrie (turmeric)
2 ml salt
250 ml cold water
5 ml white vinegar
75 ml oil for spreading

Mince filling
500 g steak or mutton mince
5 ml salt
5 ml ground jeera (cumin)
5 ml crushed dried chillis or chilli powder
5 ml crushed garlic
5 ml crushed fresh ginger
2 ml borrie (turmeric)
½ bunch green dhunia (coriander) leaves, chopped
2 onions, chopped

Filling: Wash and drain mince. Braise in a heavy frying pan until quite dry, stirring to prevent sticking and lumps forming. Add salt, jeera, chillis, garlic, ginger, borrie and dhunia leaves. Add onions and braise until well-blended. Remove from heat and cool.
Pur: Sift flour and salt into a mixing bowl. Combine water and vinegar and mix with flour to a fairly stiff mixture the consistency of bread dough. Divide into 12 balls. Working with 4 balls of dough at a time, roll each into a round the size of a large saucer (150 mm in diameter). Using your fingers, spread a little oil on each round taking care to cover it well or it will stick during cooking. Sprinkle lightly with flour. Place one round on top of the other, oily sides together. You will now have two rounds, each made up of a double layer of dough. Oil and flour the tops in the same way as before. Sandwich these together to form a single pile of four rounds, each layer of which has been oiled

and dusted with flour. Repeat with remaining balls of dough.

Gently roll out piles of rounds on a lightly floured board to a 250 mm diameter circle or oval. Turn the pastry from time to time. Place on an ungreased baking sheet and bake in a preheated oven at 200°C for about 2-3 minutes or until the pastry has puffed up slightly. Remove from oven, cut into strips 60 mm wide and 250-300 mm long, then separate into thin layers before the pastry cools. Cover with a damp cloth to prevent the pastry drying out.

Folding samoosas: Holding the strip of pastry in the left hand, pull the bottom corner across as indicated (Fig. 1). Fold upwards, adjusting edges to form a triangle with sharp corners and a pocket in which to place filling (2). Fill with 10 ml filling, then continue folding the pastry across the top of the triangle to seal off the opening. Tuck edges round to form a neat triangle (3). Seal off the small remaining edge with a paste of flour and water (4). Lightly pinch two bottom edges together to puff it up before you fry it.

To cook: Deep-fry samoosas in hot oil over a medium heat, turning once or twice to ensure that they are evenly cooked. If you fry them too quickly bubbles will appear in the pastry. When golden brown remove from oil with a slotted spoon and drain on absorbent paper. Serve immediately. Makes 48.

Vegetarian samoosas: Use any vegetable curry as a filling instead of mince. The mixture should be fairly dry and crumbly, so drain well or reduce cooking liquid.

Freezer tip
• Uncooked samoosas can be frozen for up to 6 months. There is no need to thaw before deep-frying. The filling mixture can also be frozen separately.

Microwave tip
• Instead of baking pastry rounds in the oven, first cut them into strips 60 x 250 mm then microwave on Full Power (100%) for 1-1½ minutes or until strips puff up. Separate into layers before pastry cools.

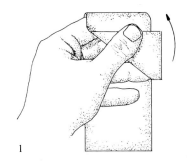

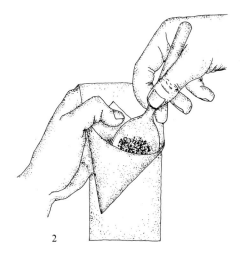

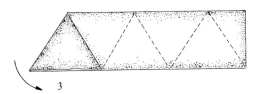

DHALTJIES

These chilli bites are the perfect party snack. You can vary this recipe by adding 250 ml sweetcorn kernels instead of spinach or by adding a grated potato.

250 ml pea or chana (yellow pea) flour
30 ml cake flour
1 onion, grated or very finely chopped
5 ml ground jeera (cumin)
5 ml ground koljander (coriander)
10 ml crushed dried chillis
5 ml salt
3 ml borrie (turmeric)
½ bunch chopped green dhunia (cori-ander) leaves
1 small green apple, grated
a few spinach leaves, shredded
5 ml baking powder
500 ml sunflower oil for deep-frying

Sift pea flour and cake flour into a fairly large mixing bowl. Add remaining ingredients, except baking powder and oil, and mix with sufficient water to make a thick batter. Stir in baking powder just before frying. Heat oil in a deep frying pan. Drop 15 ml mixture at a time into hot oil and fry until lightly browned, about 5 minutes. Turn over and brown other side. Drain on absorbent paper or in a colander and serve hot. Makes about 24.

Bhajias: Instead of shredding spinach leaves, break into 6 cm squares and dip in batter. Shallow-fry on both sides in hot oil until crisp, about 10 minutes in all. Drain well on absorbent paper and serve.

HADDOCK BALLS

An unusual savoury snack or light luncheon dish, adapted to the Malay style.

500 g smoked haddock fillets
water
2 large cooked potatoes, mashed
10 ml finely chopped fresh parsley
5 ml freshly ground white pepper
1 egg, lightly beaten
dried breadcrumbs
sunflower oil for deep-frying

Poach haddock in water to cover for about 10 minutes, drain well and flake fish. Combine with mashed potatoes, parsley and pepper and roll into balls. Dip in beaten egg, then roll in breadcrumbs. Deep-fry in hot oil until browned and crisp, about 10 minutes.

Serve hot as a snack, or as a light meal with chips, fresh tomato wedges and lemon slices. Makes 36.

SLANGETJIES

These crunchy strands are usually available at spice shops, but it is more economical to make your own.

350 ml pea or chana (yellow pea) flour
125 ml cake flour
10 ml salt
5 ml each chilli powder and jeera
30 ml sunflower oil
water
500 ml sunflower oil for deep-frying

Sift dry ingredients into a bowl. Add 30 ml oil and mix in sufficient water to make a thick paste. Push mixture through a colander with small holes or a sev machine to form spaghetti-like strands directly into hot oil and deep-fry until crisp and lightly golden. Drain well on paper towels or in a colander. Serve hot or cold. Store in an airtight container. Makes about 500 g.

Cook's tip
• A sev machine works rather like a mincer or a very large garlic press, and using one makes it far easier to handle the dough.

SPICY KEBAABS

Kebaabs are spicy hot meat balls deep-fried until golden brown. Serve with a tangy fruit chutney for easy entertaining.

500 g steak mince
5 ml crushed garlic
5 ml crushed green chillis
15 ml sunflower oil or melted butter
5 ml freshly ground black pepper
5 ml salt
2 ml ground jeera (cumin)
1 onion, grated and the juice squeezed out
1 egg, beaten
250 ml sunflower oil for deep-frying

Wash mince well and leave in a colander to drain. Mix drained mince with garlic, chillis, 15 ml oil or butter, pepper, salt, jeera, onion and egg in a mixing bowl until well-blended. Form into small balls and deep-fry in heated oil until golden brown. Drain in an absorbent paper-lined colander, then spear with toothpicks and serve with Dried fruit blatjang*. Makes 24.

Cook's tip
• The kebaabs may also be shallow-fried, for about 5 minutes on each side.

SAVOURY PIES

A favourite snack which can be served at weddings or at a buffet supper. For a thicker filling, add 100 g uncooked vermicelli to mince mixture just before adding the sago.

750 g flaky pastry
1 egg, beaten

Mince filling
500 g steak or mutton mince
2 onions, chopped
15 ml sunflower oil
5 ml crushed garlic
5 ml salt
5 ml freshly ground black pepper
2 ml grated nutmeg
2 ml ground cloves
5 ml crushed dried chillis or chilli powder
100 ml sago soaked in 125 ml water for 15 minutes
3 hard-boiled eggs, grated

Filling: Wash mince and drain well. Braise onions in heated oil until golden, 5-10 minutes. Add mince and cook for about 15 minutes, stirring, over medium heat. Add spices and cook a further 15 minutes, stirring frequently. Drain sago and add to mince mixture. Cook, stirring, until sago is transparent, about 10 minutes. Cut out pastry rounds 7,5 cm in diameter or 7,5 cm squares and place about 10 ml mince mixture in centre of half of them. Top with a little grated egg. Place remaining pastry rounds or squares on top and seal edges. Brush with beaten egg, arrange on a baking sheet and bake at 220 °C for 15 minutes. Lower temperature to 180 °C and bake a further 10 minutes or until pastry is golden brown. Serve hot. Makes 60.

Freezer tip
• Freeze unbaked savoury pies in a suitable container. There is no need to thaw them before baking in the oven. Brush with a little beaten egg, arrange on a baking sheet and bake as directed above.

Top from right to left : *Chevra (page 16), Dhaltjies, Slangetjies, Savoury pies and Samoosas (page 13).* Below from top to bottom: *Bhajias (spinach fried in batter),* Paaper *made from Samoosa* pur, *and Haddock balls.*

CHEVRA

A crunchy, spicy mixture tossed together with braised onion, peanuts and sultanas. Add 500 ml Slangetjies* for extra flavour, or add more chilli powder if you like it hot. Chevra is usually served at weddings or other special occasions such as Eid.

250 ml Post Toasties
250 ml Rice Crispies
15 ml fennel seeds
1 large potato
250 ml sunflower oil
1 small onion, thinly sliced
4 small whole green chillis
250 ml giant salted peanuts
250 ml sultanas
125 g whole mixed nuts (optional)
5 ml chilli powder
salt to taste

Combine cereals and fennel seeds in a baking dish and toast at 200 °C until golden. Coarsely grate potato into a bowl of cold water. Wash out starch and drain potato, squeezing out all moisture and fry in hot oil, stirring, until golden brown, about 8 minutes. Remove from pan, drain well and set aside. Add onion and fry until golden, 5-10 minutes. Remove from pan, drain and set aside. Dip chillis in hot oil and drain. Mix cereals, potato, onion and chillis with remaining ingredients and store in airtight containers. Makes about 1 kg.

Variation
• Colour grated potatoes with red or green food colouring before frying for a more colourful appearance.

BREAD CUPS

These crispy bread cups take only a few minutes to make. Fill with scrambled eggs for breakfast or with a variety of savoury fillings for a tasty snack.

12 slices white or brown bread, crusts removed
60 ml melted butter

Brush bread on top with melted butter and use to line well-greased muffin or deep patty pan tins. Bake at 200 °C for 10-12 minutes, or until crisp. Serve hot filled with Smoored cold meats*, Gesmoorde eier*, scrambled eggs, or Egg and shrimps*. Serves 4.

EGG CURRY

These eggs, poached in a tasty curry sauce, make a quick and easy supper dish.

1 onion, thinly sliced
30 ml sunflower oil
1 small tomato, grated or finely chopped
2 ml borrie (turmeric)
2 ml ground jeera (cumin)
2 ml ground koljander (coriander)
2 ml chilli powder
salt to taste
2 ml garam masala
8 eggs
30 ml green dhunia (coriander) leaves for garnish

Braise onion in heated oil until golden, 5-10 minutes. Add tomato and all spices except garam masala and simmer until well-blended, about 10 minutes. Stir in garam masala, then carefully break eggs into mixture, leaving a little space between them. Cook until set, scooping a little hot gravy over each while cooking. Serve garnished with dhunia leaves. Serve with Puris* or buttered bread. Serves 4.

SMOORED COLD MEATS

150 g chopped cold meats or Vienna sausages
smoor tomatoes and onions*

Add chopped cold meats or Vienna sausages to smoor tomatoes and onions and cook for about 10 minutes. Serve in Bread cups*. Serves 4.

EGG AND SHRIMPS ON TOAST

This makes a very special breakfast dish or use to fill Bread cups* for an elegant snack.

4 eggs, well beaten
15 ml milk
30 ml sunflower oil
250 g shrimps, shelled and deveined
2 ml salt
5 ml chilli powder

Combine eggs and milk. Heat oil in a frying pan and fry shrimps until they turn pink, 5-10 minutes. Add salt and chilli powder, stir and add milk and egg mixture. Cook until eggs are set but still soft and moist, about 5 minutes. Serve hot on buttered toast or use as a filling for a snackwich. Serves 4.

GESMOORDE EIER

An easy dish to make with the soft texture of scrambled eggs. Serve for breakfast or as a quick snack on toast.

15 ml sunflower oil
1 onion, thinly sliced
1 small green pepper, seeded and chopped
1 green chilli, chopped
6 eggs, well-beaten
15 ml milk
5 ml salt or garlic salt

Heat oil in a frying pan and fry onion until golden, 5-10 minutes. Add green pepper and chilli and fry for 5 minutes. Combine eggs, milk and salt and add to frying pan. Cook, stirring, until soft and moist and the texture of scrambled eggs, about 5 minutes. Serve hot on buttered toast or use as a filling for a snackwich. Serves 4-6.

SPLIT PEA SOUP

A thick, hearty soup, subtly spiced with cloves and allspice.

500 g soup meat (knuckles, neck, etc)
250 g dried split peas, soaked overnight in water to cover
5 whole cloves
5 whole allspice
2 litres water
5 carrots, grated
1 large onion, grated
2 large tomatoes, finely chopped
1 large turnip or potato, grated
100 ml chopped celery
50 ml chopped fresh parsley
salt and freshly ground black pepper to taste

Cook well-washed and drained meat with peas, cloves, allspice and 1 litre water in a fairly large saucepan for 45 minutes, or until split peas are soft. Add vegetables and remaining water, season to taste with salt and pepper and cook a further 45 minutes over medium heat. Serves 8-10.

Variation
• Use 250 g dried soup mix (barley, lentils, peas and dhal) instead of split peas.

Top: *Spicy kebaabs (page 14) with Dried fruit blatjang (page 61)*. Below left: *Split pea soup with Slangetjies (page 14)*. Below right: *Bread cups filled with Smoored cold meats*.

BEAN SOUP

An old Malay favourite, lightly spiced but without the strong flavour of chilli. If you like, serve bean soup with *kluitjies*.

250 g sugar beans
water
500 g soup meat (knuckles, neck, etc)
1 litre water
4 large carrots, grated
1 onion, grated
1 large tomato, finely chopped
2 ml freshly ground black pepper
10 ml salt, or to taste
3 whole cloves or allspice

Soak beans in water to cover for at least 3 hours. Drain and place in a large saucepan with well-washed and drained soup meat and water. Bring to boil and cook over medium heat for 40 minutes, or until meat is nearly tender. Add remaining ingredients and cook a further 30 minutes. Serves 8-10.

Variation
• Add 100 g noodles, spaghetti or macaroni 15 minutes before end of cooking time.

KLUITJIES

250 ml cake flour
pinch salt
2 ml baking powder
15 ml oil

Sift dry ingredients into a bowl. Add oil and sufficient stock from the soup to make a thick sticky dough. Mix well, then drop teaspoonsful into the hot soup. Replace lid and simmer gently for 15 minutes. Makes about 20.

SOUPS

Soups are generally served during the winter months, but also form an important part of the menu during Ramadan, when Muslims abstain from eating and drinking from sunrise to sunset.

SNOEK HEAD SOUP

My first memories of this traditional Malay dish are of my grandmother making it on a cold wintry day. Take care not to overcook the fish stock otherwise the soup may become slightly bitter.

4 large snoek heads, and leftover fish
25 ml softened butter or sunflower oil
2 large onions, thinly sliced
3 cloves garlic, crushed
125 ml thinly sliced celery
250 ml cooked rice
10 ml salt
3 litres water
5 ml freshly ground black pepper

Wash and halve snoek heads, retaining flesh behind neck. Heat butter or oil in a large saucepan and sauté the onions until golden, 5-10 minutes. Add remaining ingredients, except snoek heads, and cook, covered, for 15 minutes. Add snoek heads and cook a further 15 minutes. Serve hot. Serves 6-8.

Fish and Seafood

KINGKLIP AND PRAWN PAELLA

A special dish to serve to guests at Eid. It also makes an ideal accompaniment to Crayfish curry*.

500 g kingklip fillets, cubed
1 kg prawns, cleaned
1 kg onions, chopped
sunflower oil
200 g mushrooms, chopped
2 green peppers, seeded and chopped
2 red peppers, seeded and chopped
1 kg uncooked rice
salt
Tabasco sauce

Marinade
125 ml chilli sauce
3-4 cloves garlic, chopped
salt and freshly ground black pepper to
     taste
5 ml Tabasco sauce

Combine the marinade ingredients and marinate kingklip and prawns for about 30 minutes. Meanwhile, fry onions in a little oil in a frying pan until golden, 5-10 minutes. Add mushrooms and fry a further 5-10 minutes, or until softened. Remove onions and mushrooms from pan and set aside. Fry peppers in oil for 5 minutes, remove from pan and set aside. Transfer kingklip, prawns and marinade to frying pan and fry for 15 minutes. Boil rice until tender in boiling salted water, about 20 minutes. Drain. Layer ingredients in a large saucepan as for breyani, as follows: first rice, then onions and mushrooms (reserving some onions for decoration), then peppers, then klingklip and prawn mixture. Continue layering until all ingredients have been used, sprinkling each layer with a little salt and Tabasco sauce. Steam, covered, over medium heat for 30 minutes. Serve on its own or as an accompaniment to Crayfish curry*. Serves 10-12.

Variation
• Mussels make a good addition to this paella. Steam 250 g fresh mussels for 35-45 minutes and shell, then marinate with kingklip and prawns. If using canned mussels, add them when layering ingredients in the saucepan.

CRAYFISH CURRY

An expensive dish, but to me it is the best way to serve crayfish.

1 large crayfish or 1 kg crayfish tails, in
     shells
50 ml sunflower oil
2 large onions, thinly sliced
2 ripe tomatoes, skinned and puréed
1 green pepper, seeded and puréed
10 ml crushed garlic
5 ml crushed dried chillis
5 ml borrie (turmeric)
10 ml fish masala
5 ml ground jeera (cumin)
15 ml lemon juice
5 ml sugar
5 ml salt

Remove legs and tail if using whole crayfish. Wash well and set aside. Heat oil in a large saucepan and fry onions until golden, 5-10 minutes. Add tomatoes, green pepper, garlic and chillis and cook for 10 minutes. Add remaining spices, lemon juice, sugar and salt and cook until gravy is thick, about 10 minutes. Add crayfish (in shell), including legs and coral (if using whole crayfish) and cook over medium heat for 15 minutes. Serve hot with Dhal rice*. Serves 4.

Variation
• Add 500 g hake or kingklip fillets 10 minutes after adding crayfish and cook a further 10 minutes.

SPICED CRAYFISH SALAD

An unusual crayfish dish, spiced with ginger, coriander, thyme and nasturtium seeds. Very finely grated crayfish coral may be sprinkled over the salad as a garnish.

1 cooked crayfish
salt
freshly ground black pepper
5 ml ground ginger
1 onion, very finely chopped
6 green nasturtium seeds
5 ml fresh thyme leaves
5 ml crushed koljander (coriander) seeds
lettuce leaves
sliced hard-boiled egg for garnish
sliced cucumber for garnish

Dressing
3 egg yolks
250 ml vinegar
5 ml fresh lemon juice
45 ml ground blanched almonds

Remove flesh from large and small crayfish claws and mix with chopped flesh from tail and soft white and green flesh from inside shell. Mix well with salt and pepper to taste, ginger, onion, nasturtium seeds, thyme and koljander. *Dressing:* Beat egg yolks in vinegar and lemon juice and stir in almonds. Pour over crayfish flesh and set aside for 1 hour. Serve on lettuce leaves, garnished with hard-boiled egg slices and cucumber. Serves 4-6.

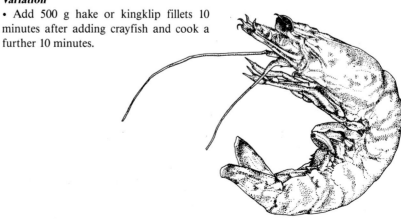

Fried kabeljou with mushroom, tomato and pepper sauce.

GRILLED PERI-PERI PRAWNS

Peri-peri, a fiery mixture of red chillis, is a flavour unique to Africa. You can vary the quantity in this recipe, depending on taste.

500 g prawns, shelled and deveined
60 ml butter

Marinade
5 ml crushed garlic
5 ml peri-peri powder
5 ml salt
30 ml lemon juice

Combine the marinade ingredients and marinate prawns in it for about 2 hours. Place prawns in a baking dish and dot with butter. Grill until pink, about 10 minutes, turning a few times and basting often with marinade. Serve with Savoury rice* and salad. Serves 4-6.

FRIED KABELJOU WITH MUSHROOM, TOMATO AND PEPPER SAUCE

A quick and easy family dish.

500 g kabeljou (cob) fillets, cut into
portions
salt and freshly ground black pepper
150 ml sunflower oil

Mushroom, tomato and pepper sauce
1 onion, finely chopped
1 green pepper, seeded and sliced
50 ml sunflower oil
2 tomatoes, skinned and chopped
200 g button mushrooms, sliced
1 small green chilli, chopped, or 5 ml
crushed dried chillis
5 ml dried mixed herbs
15 ml sugar
salt to taste

Sauce: Sauté onion and green pepper in hot oil until onion is golden, 5-10 minutes. Add tomatoes and simmer, covered, for 20 minutes. Stir in mushrooms, chilli, mixed herbs and sugar. Simmer, covered, for a further 15 minutes, then add salt to taste.

While sauce is simmering, prepare fish. Season fish lightly with salt and pepper. Heat oil in a frying pan and fry fish on both sides over low heat until lightly browned and cooked through, 10-15 minutes. Drain and place on a serving dish. Pour sauce over and serve on a bed of white rice or mashed potatoes. Serves 4.

Cook's tip
• To test if fish is done, flake one end with a fork. If done the flesh should be white and flake easily.

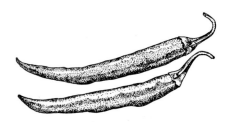

DEEP-FRIED FISH

A Saturday lunch favourite.

1 kg hake fillets
1 egg, lightly beaten
250 ml cake flour
50 ml self-raising flour
200 ml water
200 ml milk
5 ml salt
5 ml chilli powder
750 ml sunflower oil for deep-frying

Cut hake fillets into portions and set aside. Mix egg and flours to a paste in a fairly large bowl. Stir in enough water and milk until the mixture is the consistency of a pancake batter. Add salt and chilli powder and mix well. Heat oil in a deep saucepan. Dip fish portions into batter, then deep-fry in oil until golden brown, about 10 minutes. Drain on absorbent paper and serve with fried chips and tomato and lemon wedges. Serves 4-6.

Cook's tip
• The oil must not be too hot, otherwise the batter will brown before the fish is cooked through.

FRIED SNOEK

A traditional Malay dish using simple ingredients which bring out the flavour of snoek. It is customery to serve it with a garnish of onion rings and lemon wedges. I can still picture it served this way on a silver platter at my school friend's house in Caledon Street.

1 kg fresh snoek, cut into portions
5 ml salt
10 ml freshly ground black pepper
250 ml sunflower oil
2 onions, sliced into rings
lemon slices

Wash snoek well and leave in a colander to drain. Season with salt and pepper. Heat oil in a deep frying pan. Add snoek and fry for about 8 minutes on each side, or until quite brown. Remove from pan and keep warm. Fry onion rings in oil until golden, 5-10 minutes. Garnish fish with fried onion rings and lemon slices and serve with white rice and Dried red chilli blatjang*. Serves 4.

Fried snoek with onion rings and Dried red chilli blatjang (page 61).

FISH FRIKKADELS

An economical family dish which can also be served with Yellow split pea curry*.

2 slices stale white bread
water
500 g minced hake or other firm white fish
5 ml crushed garlic
1 onion, grated
1 firm ripe tomato, grated or finely
   chopped
1 egg
5 ml salt
2 ml grated nutmeg
50 ml chopped fresh parsley
2 ml white pepper
400 ml sunflower oil

Soak bread in water for 5 minutes, then squeeze out all moisture. Add to fish with remaining ingredients, except oil, and mix to bind well. Shape into patties and shallow-fry in medium hot oil for about 5 minutes on each side, or until lightly browned. Serve hot with white rice, blatjang and Tomato and onion salad*. Serves 4.

Variation
• Use 2 x 200 g cans tuna, drained and flaked, in place of minced hake.

MASALA FISH FRIED WITH BRINJALS

A spicy Indian dish, rather than a Malay one. Serve with rice or chips.

1 kg yellowtail, kabeljou (cob) or snoek,
   cut into portions
2 brinjals, sliced
sunflower oil
lemon wedges for garnish

Masala
6 cloves garlic
5 ml salt
2 green chillis
15 ml ground jeera (cumin)
30 ml lemon juice
5 ml borrie (turmeric)
15 ml sunflower oil

Pound garlic, salt and chillis to a paste in a mortar and pestle and combine with remaining masala ingredients. Smear ⅔ masala on both sides of the fish and set aside for 1 hour. Spread remainder over both sides of brinjals. Heat oil in a frying pan and fry brinjals for 5 minutes on each side, or until lightly browned. Set aside and keep warm. Fry fish for 5-6 minutes on each side in the same oil, or until cooked and golden brown. Garnish with lemon wedges and serve with chips, steamed rice or Prawn rice*.
Serves 4-5.

Cook's tip
• The garlic, salt and chillis may also be ground in a food processor or blender. This mixture keeps well in the refrigerator – prepare larger quantities and store until needed.

PICKLED FISH

As a child living in District Six, I celebrated Christmas and New Year with our neighbours. Pickled fish is a dish I always associate with the festive season. Any firm-fleshed white fish may be used instead of kabeljou or yellowtail.

2 kg kabeljou (cob) or yellowtail fillets,
   cut into portions
salt and freshly ground white pepper

Curry sauce
125 ml sunflower oil
3 large onions, thinly sliced
200 ml brown vinegar
20 ml sugar
5 ml borrie (turmeric)
10 ml curry powder
5 ml chilli powder
5 bay leaves
salt to taste

Season fish portions with salt and pepper. Heat oil in a deep frying pan and fry fish for 5 minutes on each side, or until medium brown. Remove from oil and drain. *Sauce:* Cook onions, vinegar, sugar and spices in a saucepan until well blended, 5-10 minutes. Add salt to taste. Place drained fish slices in a deep dish and cover with onion mixture. Store, covered, for 24 hours before use to allow flavour to develop. Serve with buttered bread. Serves 4-6.

SMOORSNOEK WITH CABBAGE

A very old, traditional dish which goes back a long way. In Malay households, fish is generally served on a Monday after the rich spicy foods eaten on the weekend.

1 kg dried salted snoek
water
2 onions, thinly sliced
30 ml sunflower oil
1 medium cabbage, shredded
4 cloves garlic, crushed
1 dried red chilli or 5 ml crushed dried
   chilli
5 ml sugar
4 potatoes, quartered

Soak snoek in water for 1 hour. Drain. Boil in fresh water to cover until cooked, about 15 minutes. Meanwhile, braise onions in heated oil until quite brown, about 10 minutes. Add cabbage and garlic and simmer, covered, until cabbage is lightly browned, about 15 minutes. Add chilli and sugar. Add potatoes and simmer, covered, until potatoes are cooked, about 15 minutes. Meanwhile, drain and flake snoek. Add to cabbage mixture and simmer for 15 minutes, or until flavours are well-blended. Serve with white rice and Vegetable or Lemon atjar*. Serves 8.

Variations
• Use 2 x 400 g cans smoorsnoek (available at supermarkets) instead of dried snoek. Add salt to taste.
• Use 2 x 200 g cans tuna, drained, instead of dried snoek. Add salt if needed.

SMOORED FISH WITH TOMATOES

Another quick and easy economical dish. It can also be served as a sandwich filling or on hot, buttered toast.

30 ml sunflower oil
1 large onion, thinly sliced
2 tomatoes, skinned and sliced
5 cloves garlic
5 ml salt
1 dried red chilli or 5 ml crushed dried
   chillis
5 ml sugar, or to taste
3 potatoes, quartered
2 x 200 g cans tuna, drained and flaked, or
   2 x 400 g cans smoorsnoek

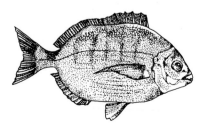

Heat oil and sauté onions until golden, 5-10 minutes. Add tomatoes and simmer until well-blended, about 10 minutes. Pound garlic and salt in a mortar and pestle and add, with chillis, sugar and potatoes, to tomato and onion mixture. Cook until potatoes are almost tender, about 10 minutes, then add fish and simmer, covered, over medium heat for 10 minutes. Serve on a bed of white rice. Serves 6.

Variation
• Use snoek roes (or other fish roes) instead of canned fish.

Left to right: ***Pickled fish and Smoorsnoek with cabbage.***

Chicken

CHICKEN CURRY

An all-time favourite. Malay curries tend to be spicier and less hot than Indian ones.

1 x 1,5 kg chicken, cut into portions
2 large onions, thinly sliced
30 ml sunflower oil
5 cloves garlic
1 piece green ginger
5 ml ground turmeric
10 ml ground jeera (cumin)
10 ml ground koljander (coriander)
5 cardamom seeds
3 pieces stick cinnamon
5 ml chilli powder
5 whole cloves
10 ml salt
375 ml water
2 large ripe tomatoes, skinned, chopped
   and puréed
3 medium potatoes, quartered

Wash and drain chicken. Meanwhile, braise onions in heated oil until golden brown, 5-10 minutes. Add chicken to onions. Pound garlic and ginger together in a mortar and pestle and add, with remaining spices and 125 ml water, to chicken mixture. Simmer, covered, for 20 minutes or until well-blended. Add tomatoes and simmer a further 10 minutes. Add remaining water and potatoes and simmer a further 10-15 minutes or until potatoes are cooked. Serve with rice or Roti* and Tomato and onion salad*. Serves 6-8.

Notes
• Add 5 ml sugar to curry, if liked.
• Purée the tomato in a food processor or blender, or rub it through a sieve.
• The garlic and ginger may also be ground in a food processor or blender.
• Tomato paste may be used instead of fresh tomatoes. Use 50 ml tomato paste mixed with 100 ml water until well-blended.

Pineapple peri-peri chicken.

DEEP-FRIED CHICKEN

Crispy crumbed chicken flavoured with spicy chilli and white pepper.

30 ml cake flour
5 ml salt
5 ml white pepper
5 ml chilli powder
1 x 1,5 kg chicken, cut into portions
1 egg, beaten
250 ml dried breadcrumbs
500 ml sunflower oil

Mix flour and spices. Dust chicken portions with flour mixture and dip them into beaten egg, then into breadcrumbs. Heat oil in a deep saucepan. Add chicken (in a frying basket, for best results) and cook for about 15 minutes. Reduce heat and cook a further 5 minutes to cook through. Remove chicken from oil and drain on absorbent paper. Serve with fresh vegetable salads and chips. Serves 6.

Cook's tip
• To test if oil is the right temperature, drop a small cube of bread into it. It should turn golden brown within 1 minute. The oil shouldn't be too hot, otherwise the chicken will brown too much before being cooked through.

PINEAPPLE PERI-PERI CHICKEN

Another Indian dish I have adapted for my family. This one has a tangy pineapple sauce which blends well with chicken.

5 ml salt
4 cloves garlic, crushed, or 5 ml garlic
   powder
8 chicken portions
30 ml cake flour
5 ml peri-peri powder
1 x 440 g can pineapple rings

Rub salt and garlic into chicken portions. Mix flour and peri-peri and sprinkle over chicken on both sides. Arrange chicken por-

tions in a greased ovenproof dish and pour syrup from pineapple over. Bake at 180 °C for about 1 hour, or until lightly browned, spooning pineapple syrup over chicken about three times and turning portions over halfway through cooking time. Arrange pineapple rings over chicken and bake a further 10-15 minutes. Serve with Savoury rice* and Vegetable atjar*. Serves 6.

POTROAST CHICKEN

Ideal for a Sunday lunch.

1 x 1,5 kg chicken, cut into portions
5 ml white pepper
5 ml crushed garlic
5 ml salt
5 ml paprika
125 ml sunflower oil

Dust chicken portions with spices and crushed garlic. Heat oil in a deep frying pan. Fry the chicken fairly quickly until browned underneath, 3-4 minutes. Turn and brown other side, then reduce heat and cook over low heat to cook right through, about 30 minutes. Serve with Almond yellow rice* and Beetroot and onion salad*. Serves 6.

Baked crumbed chicken.

BAKED CRUMBED CHICKEN

A special chicken dish to serve to guests.

1 x 1,5 kg chicken, cut into portions
125 ml flour
30 ml sesame seeds
7 ml paprika
2 ml peri-peri powder
15 ml baking powder
1 egg, lightly beaten
125 ml milk
5 cloves garlic
5 ml salt
125 ml melted butter or margarine

Wash and drain chicken. Combine flour, sesame seeds, paprika, peri-peri and baking powder in a plastic bag. Beat egg and milk in a bowl. Pound garlic with salt in a mortar and pestle and rub mixture over chicken pieces. Dip chicken pieces in egg mixture, then shake them in the plastic bag to coat evenly with flour mixture. Arrange chicken, skin side up, in an ovenproof baking dish. Pour melted margarine or butter evenly over chicken and bake at 220 °C for 40 minutes-1 hour, or until evenly browned. Serve with fresh vegetable and fruit salad and chips. Serves 4-6.

Microwave tip

• For a crisp finish, bake chicken in the oven at 220 °C for 40 minutes, then microwave on Full Power (100%) for 5 minutes before serving. If you have a combination microwave/convection oven, the whole dish can be prepared in it. Bake for 30 minutes on convection power (200 °C), then microwave on Full Power (100%) for 5 minutes.

GRILLED CHICKEN

The chicken is first baked in the oven, then grilled until golden brown.

4 cloves garlic
1 piece green ginger
5 ml salt
1 small green chilli
5 ml ground jeera (cumin)
15 ml sunflower oil
30 ml lemon juice
1 x 1,5 kg chicken, quartered or halved

Pound together garlic ginger, salt, chilli and jeera in a mortar and pestle and mix with oil and lemon juice. Alternatively combine in a food processor or blender. Rub mixture into chicken pieces and set aside for 30 minutes. Arrange chicken pieces in a greased ovenproof dish, cover with a lid or foil and bake at 200 °C for 30 minutes. Remove lid or foil and place chicken directly under grill. Baste with pan juices and grill on both sides until well-browned. Garnish with sliced lemon, tomato, pineapple and cucumber and serve with Savoury rice*. Serves 4-5.

Variations

• If you have a rotisserie, leave the chicken whole, rub it with the spice mixture and grill it for about 45 minutes or until evenly browned.
• To braai the chicken, first steam it for at least 15 minutes or cook, covered, in the microwave on Full Power (100%) for 8-10 minutes until it is parcooked. Grill for 15-20 minutes over hot coals, turning frequently.

BRAISED MASALA CHICKEN

A traditional dish, also called *gesmoorde hoender*, which I have recently discovered. I didn't think chicken could be so tasty.

1 x 1,5 kg chicken, cut into portions
125 ml sunflower oil
2 potatoes, quartered
2 onions, finely chopped
200 ml water

Masala
5 cloves garlic
piece green ginger
7 ml salt
5 ml crushed chillis
5 ml ground jeera (cumin)
10 ml leaf masala
5 ml ground cloves
30 ml lemon juice
10 ml peri-peri sauce

Wash and drain chicken. Pound together garlic, ginger and salt in a mortar and pestle. Mix to a paste with chillis, jeera, masala, cloves, lemon juice and peri-peri sauce. Rub into chicken portions and set aside. Heat oil in a saucepan and fry potatoes for about 5 minutes on each side, or until browned. Remove potatoes and set aside. Add onions to the saucepan and braise until golden, 5-10 minutes. Add chicken and cook for about 15 minutes. Add water and cook a further 10 minutes over medium heat. Add potatoes and simmer for 15 minutes or until potatoes are well-done. Serve with Smoored dhal rice*. Serves 8.

Braised masala chicken served with yellow rice, tomato and onion salad and mixed vegetable atjar.

Meat

RHUS BUKHARI

A dish from Mecca, flavoured with aromatic spices and orange peel. It can be prepared well in advance.

1 kg cubed mutton or chicken pieces
10 ml ground jeera (cumin)
10 ml ground koljander (coriander)
5 ml borrie (turmeric)
10 ml red masala
5 ml crushed dried red chillis
6 green chillis
15 ml crushed ginger
10 ml crushed garlic
5 whole cloves
3 whole allspice
3 cardamom seeds
3 pieces stick cinnamon
7 ml salt
30 ml sunflower oil
30 ml butter
2 onions, thinly sliced
3 large ripe tomatoes, grated or puréed
500 ml long grain brown rice
1 litre water
5 ml salt
thinly peeled rind of 1 orange
50 ml butter
fresh orange slices for garnishing

Combine meat with all spices and set aside. Heat oil and 30 ml butter in a large saucepan and braise onions until golden, 5-10 minutes. Add meat and spices and cook, covered, for 30 minutes. Add tomatoes and cook a further 10 minutes. Meanwhile, wash rice very well and parboil in water with 5 ml salt added, for 15 minutes. Add it to onion mixture in saucepan with meat and spices and orange rind. Dot with remaining butter and steam, covered, for 5 minutes over high heat. Turn heat down to low and steam a further 25-30 minutes. Remove orange rind and serve, garnished with fresh orange slices. Serves 6-8.

The recipe for Rhus bukhari (left), a spicy Middle Eastern dish, was brought back to the Cape by pilgrims to Mecca.

OUMENS ONDER DIE KOMBERS

Frikkadels in cabbage leaves. The mutton stew must be very soft and there must be a lot of gravy before the cabbage parcels are added.

30 ml sunflower oil
2 onions, sliced
500 g mutton, cubed
5 ml salt
5 whole cloves
2 ml freshly ground black pepper
250 ml water
1 small cabbage
5 ml ground nutmeg

Frikkadels
450 g steak mince
2 ml salt
2 ml freshly ground black pepper
2 ml ground nutmeg
5 ml crushed garlic
1 egg
1 small onion, chopped
2 slices stale white bread, soaked in water and squeezed dry

Heat oil in a fairly large saucepan. Braise onions until browned, about 15 minutes, then add meat and fry, stirring occasionally, for 15 minutes. Add spices and water and cook until meat is tender, about 45 minutes. Separate cabbage into leaves and remove veins from each. Wash leaves well, then steam until soft on top of meat, remove and set aside.

Meanwhile prepare frikkadels. Combine steak mince in a large basin with spices, egg, onion and bread. (The texture must be loose.) Place about 30 ml frikkadel mixture in centre of each cabbage leaf and roll up into parcels. Place parcels on top of stewed mutton and cook, covered, for about 30 minutes. Serve, sprinkled with nutmeg, on white rice. Serves 6-8.

MUTTABAH

A delicious meat and spinach pie with a savoury cheesy topping.

500 g flaky pastry

Filling
20 ml sunflower oil
500 g steak mince
5 ml salt
5 ml crushed dried red chillis
5 ml ground koljander (coriander)
7 spinach leaves, shredded
1 large brinjal, grated
1 onion, grated
250 ml grated Cheddar cheese

Topping
1 egg, well-beaten
150 ml milk

First make filling. Heat oil in a frying pan until lukewarm. Add mince, salt, chillis and koljander and cook for 15 minutes. Add spinach, brinjal and onion and cook a further 10 minutes. Set aside to cool. Line an ovenproof casserole dish with flaky pastry. Fill with cooled mince mixture and cover with grated cheese. Combine egg and milk well and pour over filling. Bake at 200 °C for 20-30 minutes, or until topping is set. Serve hot, with mashed potato and salads. Serves 4-6.

Spicy lamb chops, and Gem squash stuffed with braised mince.

GEM SQUASH STUFFED WITH BRAISED MINCE

4 large gem squash
20 ml sunflower oil
1 onion, thinly sliced
400 g steak mince
5 ml salt
4 whole cloves
10 ml crushed garlic
1 green chilli, chopped
1 x 410 g can baked beans in tomato

Heat oil in a large saucepan. Add onion and braise until golden brown, about 5 minutes. Wash and drain mince in a colander, then add to saucepan with salt, cloves, garlic and chilli. Cook, covered, for 30 minutes, stirring occasionally. Add beans and cook a further 10 minutes, or until well-blended. Meanwhile, halve squash and remove seeds. Stuff squash with mince and bean mixture, leaving some gravy in saucepan. Place squash in saucepan and steam, covered, for 15 minutes, or until squash is tender. Serve with white rice. Serves 4.

SPICY LAMB CHOPS

A casserole of lamb baked in a spicy yoghurt sauce.

800 g lamb loin chops
200 g button mushrooms
8 small potatoes, peeled
200 ml natural yoghurt
5 ml salt
2 green chillis, finely chopped
10 ml crushed garlic
10 ml crushed fresh ginger
10 ml ground jeera (cumin)
5 ml ground koljander (coriander)
50 ml oil

Place lamb chops, mushrooms and potatoes in a greased ovenproof dish. Combine yoghurt with remaining ingredients and pour over ingredients in dish. Bake at 200 °C for 30-45 minutes, or until meat is cooked and sauce is brown and bubbling. Serve with vegetable salad and garlic bread. Serves 6.

BRAISED STEAK WITH SWEET SOUR ONIONS

500 g rump or fillet steak
10 ml garlic steak seasoning
50 ml oil
2 onions, thinly sliced
30 ml brown vinegar
2 ml salt
1 green chilli, chopped
50 ml butter
30 ml brown sugar

Cut steak into 4-6 portions. Wash and drain steak and sprinkle with seasoning. Heat oil in deep pan. Add steak and brown on both sides, then braise, covered, on medium heat for a further 30 minutes or until tender. Move steak to side of pan. Add onions with remaining ingredients to pan and stir-fry for 7-10 minutes on high until onions are transparent and glossy. Serve with hot fried chips and mixed fruit and vegetable salad*.
Serves 4-6.

MAVROU

Spiced cubed steak served with savoury rice for easy entertaining.

1 kg cubed beef steak or boned leg
7 ml salt
7 ml ground jeera (cumin)
7 ml ground koljander (coriander)
5 ml ground barishap (fennel seeds)
5 ml crushed dried red chillis
10 ml crushed ginger
5 ml crushed garlic
3 whole cloves
3 whole allspice
3 cardamom seeds
2 pieces stick cinnamon
a few strands saffron
50 ml sunflower oil
3 large onions, thinly sliced
1 large ripe tomato, grated or finely
  chopped

Combine all spices and toss with meat. Heat oil in a large saucepan, add onions and braise until golden, 5-10 minutes. Add meat and spices and cook, covered, on medium heat for 45 minutes or until tender. Add tomato and cook a further 15 minutes, adding a pinch of sugar if desired. Serve hot on a bed of Savoury rice*. Serves 6-8.

MASALA STEAK

Tender pieces of steak smothered in a masala sauce.

30 ml sunflower oil
2 large onions, thinly sliced
2 tomatoes, chopped
10 ml crushed fresh ginger
10 ml crushed garlic
2 ml borrie (turmeric)
10 ml steak masala
1 kg rump steak, cut into 10 cm pieces
5 ml salt

Heat oil and braise onions until golden brown, about 5 minutes. Add tomatoes, ginger, garlic, borrie and masala and cook for about 15 minutes, or until well-blended. Add steak and salt and cook over medium heat until steak is tender, about 30 minutes. Serve with chips and vegetable salad. Serves 6-8.

From top to bottom: *Masala steak and Mavrou served with gesmoorde rice.*

KOTELETTE

Lamb chops in breadcrumbs covered with an onion-flavoured sauce which makes this very different from other Malay dishes.

1 kg lamb leg chops
5 ml salt
5 ml freshly ground black pepper
150 ml water
2 eggs, lightly beaten
250 ml dry breadcrumbs
200 ml sunflower oil

Onion gravy
1 onion, thinly sliced
30 ml cake flour
30 ml water
5 ml lemon juice
15 ml chopped fresh parsley

Season chops with salt and pepper and steam in water in a saucepan over medium heat until tender, 35-45 minutes. Remove from saucepan and reserve liquid for gravy. Dip chops in beaten egg and then coat in breadcrumbs. Heat oil in a frying pan and fry chops for about 7 minutes on each side, or until golden brown. *Onion gravy:* Add onion to reserved liquid in saucepan and cook until transparent, about 5 minutes. Mix flour to a paste with water and add to saucepan with lemon juice and parsley. Add fried chops to gravy, spooning gravy over them, or serve chops and gravy separately, accompanied by mashed potatoes and cooked beetroot. Serves 6.

KEBAABS

A kind of 'Scotch egg'.

30 ml sunflower oil
1 large onion, thinly sliced
2 ml borrie (turmeric)
5 ml curry powder
10 ml red masala
500 g steak mince
3 slices stale white bread, soaked in water
    and squeezed dry
5 ml salt
1 egg, lightly beaten
5 ml crushed garlic
5 ml crushed fresh ginger
5 ml ground barishap
10 ml ground jeera (cumin)
5 hard-boiled eggs, quartered

Heat oil in a frying pan and braise onions until light brown, about 5 minutes. Add bor-rie, curry powder and masala and mix well. Meanwhile, combine steak mince, bread, salt, egg, garlic, ginger, barishap and jeera in a large bowl. Pour hot onion mixture over mince mixture and combine well. Take about 30 ml mince mixture in your palm, flatten it and place an egg quarter in the centre. Fold mince mixture over egg, to enclose it completely. Repeat until all ingredients have been used. Shallow-fry in heated oil for 7 minutes on each side or place on a greased baking sheet and bake for 30 minutes at 180 °C. Serve hot with Almond yellow rice*, mashed potatoes and Beetroot and onion salad*. Serves 6-8.

FILLET IN BREADCRUMBS

600 g steak fillet, cut in 1 cm thick slices
200 ml cake flour
2 eggs, well-beaten
200 ml dried breadcrumbs
150 ml sunflower oil

Marinade
5 ml crushed chillis
5 ml salt
5 ml crushed garlic
2 ml freshly ground black pepper
30 ml lemon juice

Wash meat well and drain in a colander. Combine marinade ingredients and rub into fillet slices on both sides. Set aside for 1 hour. Dip each piece of fillet first in flour, then in eggs and finally in breadcrumbs. Heat oil in a large frying pan and fry fillet slices for 10 minutes on each side, or until golden brown. Drain on absorbent paper before serving with lightly cooked mixed vegetables and mashed potato or Smoored rice*. Serves 4.

POT ROAST LEG OF LAMB

A leg of lamb seasoned generously with crushed chillis, ginger and garlic.

2 kg leg of lamb
sunflower oil
200 ml water
30 ml cake flour

Stuffing
10 ml salt
5 ml freshly ground black pepper
5 ml crushed chillis
5 ml crushed fresh ginger
10 ml crushed garlic
30 ml lemon juice
30 ml sunflower oil

Combine all stuffing ingredients. Wash meat well and make deep gashes in it. Fill gashes with stuffing mixture. Heat a little oil in a deep saucepan and brown leg on all sides, uncovered. Add water and roast, covered, over medium heat for 1 hour or until meat is well-done. Remove leg from saucepan. Stir flour into pan juices and bring to boil, stirring, to form a gravy. Slice meat and pour gravy over before serving with roast potatoes, Almond yellow rice* and salads. Serves 8-10.

Variation
• Add 6 small potatoes and 8 small carrots to pan juices after removing leg and cook until tender, about 15 minutes, before making gravy. Keep meat warm while doing so.

MALAY BRAAI MARINADE

On weekends and public holidays we love to braai. This recipe makes a very tasty meat marinade.

10 ml crushed garlic
10 ml crushed fresh ginger
10 ml ground koljander (coriander)
30 ml sunflower oil
30 ml fruit chutney
5 ml salt
5 ml crushed chillis
30 ml lemon juice

Combine all ingredients to a paste and use to smear on both sides of meat before braaiing or grilling. Makes 130 ml.

Denningvleis on almond yellow rice.

DENNINGVLEIS

There is no other name in any language for this popular Malay dish. At first glance it looks like lamb stew, but when eaten it has a lingering, spicy undertone.

1 kg leg of lamb
500 g onions, thinly sliced

Marinade
5 cloves garlic, crushed
5 ml crushed chillis
5 ml salt
2 ml freshly ground black pepper
3 bay leaves
5 whole allspice
15 ml sugar, or to taste
20 ml brown vinegar

Wash meat very well. Bone meat and cut into 5 cm chunks. Combine the marinade ingredients and coat meat in it. Set aside for 1 hour. Combine onions and meat in a large saucepan and cook, covered, over medium heat until meat is well-done, about 45 minutes. If meat gets too dry, add a little water (no more than 250 ml). Serve meat hot with boiled squash, mashed potatoes and Almond yellow rice*. Serves 4-6.

Cook's tip
• Traditionally, tamarind was used instead of vinegar for the marinade. Soak 30 ml tamarind in 50 ml water and add to marinade ingredients.

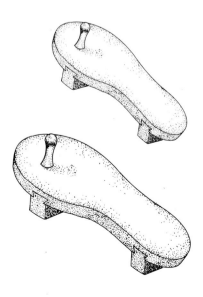

TRADITIONAL SOSATIES

Another very old but well loved Malay dish from the Indonesian island of Java. The addition of herbs in this recipe imparts an unusual flavouring to the spicy marinade.

1 kg leg of lamb, boned and cubed
500 g onions, thinly sliced
125 ml sunflower oil

Marinade
4 orange or bay leaves
5 ml fresh thyme sprigs or 2 ml dried
10 ml fresh sage or 5 ml dried
15 ml curry powder
60 ml vinegar or lemon juice
50 ml sugar, or to taste
10 ml crushed garlic

Combine the marinade ingredients and marinate meat and onions for at least 2 hours, but preferably overnight. Thread cubed meat onto sosatie sticks and fry on all sides in heated oil, for about 20 minutes altogether. Remove from pan and add onions and marinade mixture. Cook until onions are transparent, about 5 minutes. Return sosaties to pan and cook a further 20 minutes. Serve with Smoored rice* and mashed potatoes. Serves 6.

Braaied sosaties: Grill sosaties over medium coals until tender yet crisp. Heat marinade separately for a tasty sauce.

FRIKKADELS WITH SMOOR TOMATO AND ONION

3 slices stale white bread, crusts removed
water
500 g steak mince
5 ml freshly ground black pepper
5 ml salt
1 large egg
1 onion, grated
5 ml ground koljander (coriander)
5 ml crushed garlic
300 ml sunflower oil

Soak bread in water for 10 minutes, then squeeze dry. Add to mince and remaining ingredients, except oil, and mix to combine well. Shape into frikkadels and shallow-fry in medium hot oil, for 7 minutes on each side, or until browned. Serve with Smoor tomato and onion* and mashed potato. Serves 4-6.

SOSATIE CHOPS

This is a modern version of the traditional sosatie. Try it. It is superb, especially for slimmers as it's oil free.

1 kg lamb chops
500 g onions, thinly sliced

Marinade
10 ml crushed garlic
3 bay leaves
3 whole cloves
1 green chilli, finely chopped
5 ml borrie (turmeric)
30 ml curry powder
45 ml sugar
5 ml salt
60 ml lemon juice or vinegar

Combine the marinade ingredients and marinate chops for 1 hour. Place meat and marinade in a saucepan with onions and cook, covered, over medium heat for 45 minutes – 1 hour, or until meat is tender. Serve with boiled squash and potatoes. Serves 6.

BOBOTIE

A light-textured curried meat loaf topped with a golden savoury custard.

2 slices stale white bread, crusts removed
water
30 ml sunflower oil
1 onion, thinly sliced
2 ml ground cloves
5 ml crushed garlic
5 ml salt
10 ml curry powder
5 ml borrie (turmeric)
500 g steak mince
2 eggs
30 ml hot water
20 ml lemon juice
30 ml sugar
4 bay or lemon leaves for garnish

Topping
1 egg, lightly beaten
150 ml milk

Soak bread in water for 10 minutes, then squeeze dry. Heat oil in a large frying pan and braise onion until golden, 5-10 minutes. Add cloves, garlic, salt, curry powder and borrie and simmer for 5 minutes. Add to mince with eggs, hot water, lemon juice and sugar and mix to combine well. Spoon mix-

ture into a well-greased ovenproof dish and bake at 160 °C for 40 minutes, or until golden brown. Remove from oven. Beat egg and milk well and pour over bobotie. Add bay or lemon leaves and bake a further 5-10 minutes at 180 °C. Serve with Almond yellow rice* or boiled vegetables. Serves 6.

SPICY COTTAGE PIE

500 g steak mince
1 large onion, thinly sliced
10 ml crushed garlic
5 ml freshly ground black pepper
5 ml salt
2 ml ground cloves
2 ml ground nutmeg
50 ml sago, soaked in 100 ml water for
  30 minutes
500 g mashed potatoes
3 hard-boiled eggs, sliced
1 egg, well-beaten

Combine steak mince and onion in a saucepan and braise slowly, covered, for 30 minutes. Add garlic, pepper, salt, cloves and nutmeg and cook a further 10 minutes. Add sago and cook over medium heat for about 15 minutes, or until sago is translucent. Meanwhile make mashed potatoes (see below). Transfer mince from saucepan to a greased ovenproof dish. Layer hard-boiled egg slices on top and cover with mashed potatoes. Pour over beaten egg and bake at 200 °C for 15 minutes. Serve with lightly steamed vegetables and Beetroot and onion salad*. Serves 6.

Variation
• Use 400 g gheema (cubed steak) and 1 ox kidney, cubed, instead of steak mince.

Mashed potatoes: Boil 500 g potatoes, cubed, in boiling salted water for 15-20 minutes, or until soft enough to mash. Add 50 ml butter, 100 ml milk, 2 ml salt and 5 ml baking powder and mash until soft and fluffy.

From top to bottom: ***Frikkadels with smoor tomato and onion and Sosatie chops on yellow rice with raisins.***

Meat Delicacies

PENSLAWER

A tripe curry, unusual in flavour and well worth the effort.

1 kg cleaned tripe
salted water
30 ml sunflower oil
3 large onions, thinly sliced
1 tomato, grated
10 ml crushed garlic
5 ml borrie (turmeric)
5 ml ground koljander (coriander)
4 bay leaves
1 green chilli
a few strands saffron (optional)
3 whole cloves
10 ml roasted masala
5 ml sugar
salt to taste
200 ml natural yoghurt

Cook tripe in salted water to cover until very soft and tender, about 2 hours. Drain and reserve liquid. Heat oil in a heavy-based saucepan and braise onions and garlic until golden brown, 5-10 minutes. Add tomato, spices, sugar and sufficient reserved liquid to make a gravy. Cut tripe into strips about 5 cm long and 1 cm wide and add to mixture in saucepan. Cook, covered, over medium heat until tripe and gravy are well-blended, about 15 minutes. Add salt to taste and yoghurt. Cook for an additional 10 minutes, but do not boil or yoghurt will curdle. Serve with white rice and atjars. Serves 6.

Variations
• Make frikkadels as described in Pootjies tamatie* recipe and add, with 200 ml water, when adding tripe. Do not stir mixture once frikkadels have been added.
• Add 250 g frozen mixed carrots and peas when adding tripe.

Cook's tip
• Buy only well-cleaned tripe. Cut into smaller pieces and soak in boiling water to cover for 15 minutes. Lift each piece out and scrape well with a knife until completely clean. Rinse well in cold water. Doing this will ensure that the tripe is white.

OX TROTTER AND DRIED PEAS

500 g dried peas
1 litre water
1 ox trotter, well-cleaned
salted water
30 ml sunflower oil
2 large onions, thinly sliced
10 ml crushed garlic
3 peppercorns
5 ml freshly ground black pepper
5 ml salt
30 ml butter
2 ml ground nutmeg

Soak peas overnight in water to cover. Place in a large saucepan, add 1 litre water and cook until soft and mushy, about 30 minutes. Purée in a blender or food processor, or rub through a sieve, to obtain a smooth texture. Meanwhile, cook trotter in salted water to cover until tender, about 2½ hours. Drain well. Heat oil in a large saucepan and braise onions until golden, 5-10 minutes. Add cooked trotter, garlic, peppercorns, pepper and salt and cook for 10 minutes. Add peas and cook a further 15-20 minutes, until well-blended. Just before serving, dot with butter and sprinkle with nutmeg. Serve with white rice and atjars. Serves 8.

POTROAST SHEEP TONGUES

One of the tastiest of the meat delicacies.

4 sheep tongues
boiling water
250 ml water
3 whole cloves
3 whole pimentoes
5 ml salt
3 ml coarsely ground black pepper
5 ml crushed garlic
3 ml chilli powder
50 ml sunflower oil
4 medium potatoes (optional)

Pour boiling water over tongues and soak for about 10 minutes. Remove tongues from water one by one and scrape very well with the back of a knife. Slit tongues in half and rinse under cold water. Combine tongues and 250 ml water with whole cloves and pimentoes and cook over medium heat for 1½ hours, or until tongues are soft. Make a paste with salt, black pepper, garlic and chilli powder. Rub into tongues and return to saucepan with sunflower oil. Brown over medium heat until flavours are well-blended, about 15 minutes, stirring occasionally. Add potatoes and cook until tender, 15-20 minutes. Serve with boiled squash and Almond yellow rice*. Serves 4.

TRIPE IN BATTER

Golden brown squares of tripe fried in a crispy batter. It looks like fish 'n chips, but tastes quite different.

1 kg tripe, cleaned
salted water
10 ml salt
5 ml freshly ground white pepper
200 ml sunflower oil

Batter
1 egg
250 ml milk
30 ml self-raising flour
125 ml cake flour

Wash tripe very well and drain. Cut into smaller pieces. Boil in salted water to cover until very tender, about 2½ hours. Leave to cool, then cut into 6 cm squares. Season with salt and pepper. *Batter:* Combine ingredients to form a smooth batter. Dip tripe in batter and shallow-fry in hot oil for 5 minutes on each side, or until crisp. Drain on absorbent paper and serve hot with chips and salads. Serves 6.

POOTJIES TAMATIE

Sheep trotters and tomato cooked until the mixture resembles a gelatinous tomato bredie.

12 sheep trotters, well-cleaned
salted water
30 ml sunflower oil
3 large onions, thinly sliced
1 kg ripe tomatoes, grated or very finely chopped
30 ml tomato paste
100 ml water
5 ml crushed dried chillis
15 ml crushed garlic
10 ml salt
60 ml sugar, or to taste

Boil trotters in salted water to cover in a deep saucepan until very soft, 1½-2 hours. Heat oil in another large saucepan and braise onions until golden, 5-10 minutes. Add tomatoes, tomato paste mixed with 100 ml water, chillis and garlic and cook until sauce is thick, 20-30 minutes. Add trotters with cooking liquid, salt and sugar to tomato mixture and cook, covered, over medium heat until flavours are well-blended, 15-20 minutes. Serve with white rice. Serves 8-10.

Cook's tip

• For tender trotters, cook in a pressure cooker at 100 kPa for 45 minutes.

Tamatie frikkadels: Omit trotters and add frikkadels instead. To make frikkadels, combine 500 g steak mince, 5 ml salt, 1 egg, 5 ml freshly ground white pepper, 2 ml grated nutmeg, 5 ml crushed garlic, 3 slices white bread soaked in water and squeezed dry and 1 grated onion. Form into balls and add to sauce.

FRIED LIVER AND ONIONS

An old favourite with a lot of people. The green chilli gives it a bit of a bite, while the sugar and vinegar gives a slight sweet-sour taste. Use plenty of onion to thicken the gravy.

500 g lamb's liver, cleaned
water
7 ml salt
5 ml freshly ground black pepper
100 ml milk
150 ml cake flour
150 ml sunflower oil
1 large onion, thinly sliced
1 green chilli, chopped
15 ml sugar
30 ml brown vinegar

Soak liver in water to cover for 30 minutes. Drain and remove membrane, then slice liver thinly. Season with 5 ml salt and pepper and pour milk over. Soak for 30 minutes. Remove liver slices from milk and coat lightly in flour. Heat oil in a frying pan and fry liver for 5-10 minutes on each side, or until lightly browned. Remove from pan, drain and keep warm. Add the sliced onion, chilli, sugar, vinegar and remaining salt to pan. Stir in onion and braise mixture until onion is golden, 5-10 minutes. Return liver to pan and cook 10-15 minutes, adding 100 ml hot water if more gravy is needed. Serve with mashed potatoes and vegetables. Serves 4-6.

Penslawer, a fragrant tripe curry.

Bredies and Breyani

BREDIE

Bredie is an old Cape name for a dish of meat and vegetables stewed together so that the flavours intermingle and it is almost impossible to separate the one from the other. The unique flavour of a bredie is determined by the kind of vegetables added, hence the name tomato, bean, cauliflower or sugar bean bredie. More than one vegetable may be added in addition to onions and potatoes. The potato also helps to thicken the gravy. Although almost any vegetable may be used in a bredie, the meat is almost always lamb or mutton. Mutton is ideal for bredies as the long slow simmering tenderizes it and brings out the full flavour.

Recipes for bredies have been handed down through many generations and they have changed very little in character over the years. The flavour is so delicious that there is little need for additional herbs and spices.

CAULIFLOWER BREDIE

A surprisingly tasty bredie to make in the winter months. Sprinkle a little grated nutmeg over the bredie just before serving.

2 onions, thinly sliced
30 ml sunflower oil
1 kg mutton thick rib
7 ml salt
5 whole cloves
2 whole allspice
1 green chilli or 5 ml crushed dried chillis
10 ml sugar
150 ml water
1 large cauliflower, broken into florets
3 potatoes, quartered

Braise onions in heated oil until golden, 5-10 minutes. Add meat and simmer slowly for about 45 minutes, or until meat is well-browned. Add salt, cloves, allspice, chillis, sugar and water. Bring to the boil and simmer for about 10 minutes or until flavours are well-blended. Add cauliflower and potatoes and cook until vegetables are soft, about 20 minutes. Serve with white rice and sambals or atjars. Cucumber and onion salad goes particularly well with this bredie. Serves 6.

Cabbage bredie: Use 1 medium cabbage, finely shredded, instead of cauliflower and omit water, as cabbage draws a lot of water.

WORTEL EN RAAP BREDIE

Carrot and turnip bredie. If you like, omit turnips and add 3 cloves with red chillis.

20 ml sunflower oil
2 onions, thinly sliced
600 g mutton or lamb, cubed
5 ml sugar (optional)
1 small bunch carrots, sliced
3 turnips, sliced
salt to taste
5 ml crushed dry red chillis
250 ml water

Heat oil and braise onions until golden, 5-10 minutes. Add well-washed and drained meat and braise until dark brown and nearly tender, 35-40 minutes. Sugar may be added at this point to brown meat quickly. Add carrots and turnips, salt, chillis and water and cook over medium heat until well-blended and meat is tender, about 20 minutes. Serve hot with rice and atjars. Serves 4-6.

Wortel en ertjie bredie: Use 200 g frozen peas instead of turnips and add 10 minutes before end of cooking time. Add 3 potatoes, halved, with carrots. Sprinkle about 25 ml chopped fresh parsley over and dot with 25 ml butter just before serving. This bredie is sometimes called *Kifayahkos* as it is often served at funerals.

SAGO AND PARSLEY BREDIE

Another traditional bredie and popular with the old folk who find it easy to digest. Take care to simmer the meat slowly as rapid boiling will toughen it. The sago thickens the gravy and the parsley adds flavour along with allspice and cloves.

30 ml sunflower oil
2 onions, thinly sliced
600 g mutton or lamb, cubed
10 ml crushed garlic
5 whole cloves
5 whole allspice
5 ml freshly ground black pepper
5 ml salt, or to taste
2 ml ground nutmeg
200 ml water
125 ml sago, soaked in 250 ml water for 30 minutes
30 ml chopped fresh parsley

Heat oil in a large saucepan and braise onions until golden, 5-10 minutes. Add well-washed and drained meat and simmer slowly for 45 minutes, or until meat is nearly tender. Add garlic, cloves, allspice, pepper, salt and nutmeg and cook another 15 minutes. Stir in water, then add soaked sago and parsley and cook until sago is transparent, about 15 minutes, adding more water if desired. Serve with mashed potatoes or white rice. Serves 6.

Microwave tip
• Combine soaked sago and 500 ml water in casserole dish and microwave for 1 minute on Full Power (100%), then on Medium High (70%) for 2 minutes. Add to bredie with parsley and cook a further 8-10 minutes before serving.

Wortel and raap bredie, a traditional Malay dish served with atjar.

SPLIT PEA BREDIE

The flavour of this bredie will improve if it is made a day or two in advance.

250 g yellow or green split peas
30 ml sunflower oil
2 onions, thinly sliced
600 g mutton or lamb, cubed
5 ml salt, or to taste
2 dried red chillis or 10 ml crushed dried red chillis
200 ml water

Soak split peas overnight in water to cover. Heat oil in a large saucepan and braise the onions until golden, 5-10 minutes. Add washed and drained meat and cook a further 40-50 minutes, or until meat is tender. Add salt, chilli, peas and soaking water, plus 200 ml water and cook a further 15 minutes, or until peas are soft and cooked through. Serve with Dhal rice* and salads. Serves 4-6.

Microwave tip

• Microwave soaked split peas with 750 ml water in a covered casserole dish for 8 minutes on Full Power (100%), then 15 minutes on Medium High (70%). Continue as described above.

TOMATO BREDIE

Ripe, red tomatoes are best for this dish. If you have to use canned tomatoes or less than ripe tomatoes, add 15-30 ml tomato paste for extra flavour.

2 large onions, thinly sliced
30 ml sunflower oil
1 kg mutton knuckles, chopped
1 kg ripe tomatoes, skinned and chopped or puréed
4 cloves garlic
5 ml salt
1 dry red chilli, crushed
30 ml tomato paste
4 medium potatoes, quartered
30 ml sugar, or to taste

Braise onions in heated oil until golden, 5-10 minutes. Add meat and simmer over medium heat for 30-40 minutes, stirring from time to time. Add tomatoes, garlic crushed to a paste with salt, chilli and tomato paste and simmer a further 20 minutes. Add potatoes and cook until tender, about 15 minutes. Add sugar and cook a further 5 minutes. Serve with white rice and vegetable atjar. Serves 8.

Cook's tip

• Add the sugar last, as the potatoes take a long time to cook if sugar is added first.

Microwave tip

• Microwave quartered potatoes with 50 ml water for 5 minutes on Full Power (100%). Add to bredie and cook for 5 minutes before adding sugar. This will reduce total cooking time by about 15 minutes.

SUGAR BEANS BREDIE

250 g sugar beans
20 ml sunflower oil
1 large onion, thinly sliced
500 g mutton or lamb, cubed
10 ml crushed garlic
5 ml salt, or to taste
1 green chilli, chopped
20 ml tomato paste
200 ml water
5 ml sugar

Soak sugar beans overnight in cold water. Drain and cook in water to cover until fairly soft, about 1 hour. Meanwhile, heat oil in a large saucepan and braise onions until golden, 5-10 minutes. Add well-washed and drained meat with garlic, salt and chilli and cook a further 40-45 minutes, or until meat is tender but not too brown. Add sugar beans and cook a further 10 minutes. Add tomato paste mixed with water and sugar and cook a further 10-15 minutes, or until sauce is well-blended. Serve with white rice and atjars. Serves 6.

Microwave tip

• Add 750 ml hot water to soaked and drained beans and microwave, covered, for 10 minutes on Full Power (100%), then a further 30-40 minutes on Medium (50%).

SNYBOONTJIES BREDIE

30 ml sunflower oil
2 large onions, thinly sliced
1 kg mutton or lamb, cubed
10 ml salt, or to taste
20 ml sugar
5 ml crushed dried chillis
1 kg green beans, sliced diagonally
3 potatoes, halved

Heat oil in a large saucepan and braise the onions until lightly browned, 5-10 minutes. Add well-washed and drained meat and braise until browned, about 45 minutes.

Add salt, sugar and chillis, and top with green beans. Cook, covered, for 15 minutes, then add potatoes and cook over medium heat until potatoes are tender, about 15 minutes, adding water if more gravy is required. Serve with white rice and Cucumber and onion salad*. Serves 6.

Pumpkin bredie: Omit potatoes and green beans and add 1 kg peeled pumpkin or butternut, cubed, after adding salt, sugar and chillis. Add 5 ml crushed garlic, 2 pieces stick cinnamon and a little more sugar at the same time.

MUTTON BREYANI

1 kg mutton or lamb, cubed
10 ml crushed fresh ginger
10 ml crushed garlic
5 ml salt
250 ml brown lentils
500 ml water
500 g long grain brown rice or basmati rice
250 ml sunflower oil
300 ml hot water
6 potatoes
3 large onions, thinly sliced
50 g butter
5 ml salt
6 hard-boiled eggs, halved, for garnish

Marinade
3 pieces stick cinnamon
5 cardamom seeds
2 green chillis
2 ml borrie (turmeric)
5 ml red masala
30 ml breyani masala
5 whole cloves
5 pimentos
a few strands saffron
1 large tomato, grated or finely chopped
250 ml buttermilk

Wash and drain meat in a colander. Rub ginger, garlic and salt into meat. Combine marinade ingredients and marinate meat in it for about 3 hours. Cook lentils in water for 20 minutes, or until tender. Rinse and drain in a colander. Wash rice until water runs clear and drain off most of the water. Heat 50 ml oil in a large frying pan over medium heat and add rice. Toss to coat well. Add 100 ml hot water and cook, covered, for 5 minutes on medium. Remove from stove.

Heat remaining oil in a large deep saucepan and fry potatoes on all sides until browned, about 4 minutes. Remove and set aside. Add onions and braise until brown

Mutton breyani, an aromatic dish, is often accompanied by weak black tea to offset the richness.

and crisp, 7-8 minutes. Remove about a quarter of the onions from pan and reserve. Add meat and spices to remaining onions and cook, covered, for 30 minutes. Remove meat from saucepan and keep warm. Layer potatoes in the same saucepan, then layer other ingredients as follows: Sprinkle half rice over potatoes, then sprinkle half the salt over the rice. Arrange meat mixture over rice. Sprinkle lentils over, then remaining rice and salt. Top with reserved onions. Dot with butter and sprinkle with remaining hot water. Close saucepan, sealing lid tightly. Cook on high for 5 minutes, then simmer for 45 minutes-1 hour on low. Do not open saucepan. Top breyani with halved hard-boiled eggs and serve with atjars and Tomato and onion salad*. Serves 10.

Chicken breyani: Use chicken pieces instead of lamb, and marinate for 2 hours only.

MINCE AND MIXED VEGETABLE BREYANI

500 ml long grain brown rice
15 ml salt
7 ml borrie (turmeric)
2 onions, thinly sliced
500 g steak mince
3 cloves
3 cardamom seeds
2 pieces stick cinnamon
10 ml crushed fresh ginger
5 ml crushed garlic
10 ml ground jeera (cumin)
10 ml ground koljander (coriander)
5 ml chilli powder
30 ml tomato paste or 60 ml grated or
finely chopped tomato
250 g frozen mixed vegetables
60 ml butter
150 ml water

Cook rice in water to cover with 10 ml salt and 2 ml borrie until nearly tender, about 20 minutes. Rinse and drain in a colander. Combine onions, mince, cloves, cardamoms, stick cinnamon, ginger and garlic in a large saucepan. Cook over medium heat for 30 minutes, then add jeera, koljander, chilli powder, remaining borrie and salt and tomato. Cook a further 10 minutes, or until spices are well-blended. Add the mixed vegetables and cook for 5 minutes. Layer half rice in a large saucepan, top with mince mixture and remaining rice. Dot with butter and sprinkle water over. Cook, tightly covered, for 5 minutes on high and then for 30 minutes on medium. Serve with salads and atjars. Serves 6.

Microwave tip

• Layer ingredients in a casserole dish as described above and microwave, covered, on Medium (50%) for 15-20 minutes to finish cooking the breyani.

FRIKKADEL BREYANI

100 ml sunflower oil
500 ml long grain rice
10 ml salt
3 whole cloves
3 cardamom seeds
2 pieces stick cinnamon
60 ml butter
1 onion, thinly sliced
100 ml hot water

Frikkadels
500 g lean steak mince
1 onion, grated
1 egg
5 ml salt
5 ml crushed garlic
30 ml crushed green dhunia (coriander)
    leaves
5 ml ground jeera (cumin)
15 ml fennel seeds
2 ml ground cinnamon
10 ml crushed green chillis

Combine frikkadel ingredients and shape into small balls. Fry in 75 ml heated oil until browned and pan is dry. Remove and set aside. Boil rice in water to cover with salt, cloves, cardamom seeds and cinnamon, for about 20 minutes. Drain and leave in colander. Heat 25 ml oil and 30 ml butter in a large saucepan and braise onions until golden brown, about 5 minutes. Remove half and set aside. Add half rice to saucepan, place frikkadels on top and then remaining rice. Sprinkle reserved onions over rice, dot with remaining butter and sprinkle with hot water. Close saucepan tightly and cook for 5 minutes on high, then on medium for 30-35 minutes. Do not open saucepan during cooking. Serve with atjars and salads. Serves 6-8.

Microwave tip
• Layer prepared ingredients in exactly the same way in a casserole dish and microwave, covered, on Medium (50%) for 15-20 minutes to finish cooking the breyani. The rice is much fluffier if cooked this way.

Cook's tip
• The secret to keeping the grains of rice separate is to wash it well until the water runs clear, then coat it in oil before cooking it.

FISH BREYANI

500 g long grain rice
250 ml lentils
sunflower oil
5 medium potatoes
3 large onions, thinly sliced
1 kg kabeljou (cob), snoek or other firm
    white fish
30 ml buttermilk
1 tomato, skinned and chopped
2 whole green chillis
5 ml ground jeera (cumin)
5 whole cloves
5 whole allspice
5 cardamom seeds
2 pieces stick cinnamon
60 ml butter
250 ml hot water

Masala
6 cloves garlic
5 ml salt
2 green chillis
15 ml jeera (cumin)
30 ml lemon juice
5 ml borrie (turmeric)
15 ml sunflower oil

Boil rice in salted water until half done, about 10 minutes. Rinse in cold water and drain. Boil lentils separately in salted water until half done, about 15 minutes. Rinse in cold water and drain. Heat 250 ml oil in a saucepan and brown potatoes quickly on all sides, 3-4 minutes, then set aside. Braise onions in same oil until golden, 5-10 minutes. Drain and reserve half and set remainder aside in saucepan.

To make masala, pound garlic, salt and chillis in a mortar and pestle and combine with other ingredients. Smear over fish and fry fish separately in oil until firm and lightly browned, about 8 minutes on each side. Remove from pan and keep warm. Combine buttermilk, tomato, chillis, jeera, cloves, allspice, cardamom seeds and cinnamon. Add to onions in saucepan and simmer for 10 minutes.

Arrange potatoes in base of a very large saucepan. Sprinkle half the cooked rice over and arrange fish slices on top. Spoon onion and spice mixture on top and then lentils. Add remaining rice, then top with reserved onions and dot with butter. Sprinkle water over and close saucepan tightly. Steam over high heat for 5 minutes, then reduce heat and simmer over low heat for 30 minutes. Serve hot with Tomato and onion salad* or sambals of your choice. Serves 8.

Cook's tip
• It is essential that the lid of the saucepan fits tightly. If it doesn't, place a large piece of greaseproof paper or foil over the saucepan before putting on the lid. For best results, leave breyani to cook undisturbed for entire cooking time.

BREYANI

A popular Indian dish adapted by the Cape Malays and usually served on religious festivals and other special occasions such as weddings. A breyani is very often made in three stages. First the rice is parboiled in salted water. Lentils are also sometimes used and they, too, are parboiled. Then mutton, fish or chicken is cut into serving pieces and simmered in another pot with chopped onion, root ginger, garlic and a liberal mixture of aromatic spices until the meat is nearly cooked. Finally, the dish is assembled by layering the rice and lentils alternately with the spicy meat mixture in a cast iron pot or in a suitable large ovenproof casserole dish. The pot or casserole is tightly covered and the mixture is allowed to simmer slowly until done. The lid is not removed until the moment of serving, so as to retain the fragrant aroma. A breyani is the ideal way to feed a large crowd as it can be assembled beforehand in a large container and the longer it cooks, the more flavour it seems to absorb.

TUNA BREYANI

100 ml sunflower oil
3 potatoes, sliced
50 ml butter
1 large onion, thinly sliced
5 ml chilli powder
5 ml ground jeera (cumin)
250 g frozen mixed vegetables
750 ml cooked long grain rice
2 x 200 g cans tuna, drained and flaked
100 ml hot water
3 hard-boiled eggs, quartered

Heat oil in a frying pan and fry potato slices for about 5 minutes on each side, or until golden brown. Drain and set aside. Melt butter in a saucepan and fry onion until golden, 5-10 minutes. Add spices and mixed vegetables and cook a further 10 minutes.

Tuna breyani served with Lemon atjar (page 61) makes an excellent light meal or starter.

Layer 375 ml rice in a large saucepan, top with tuna, potatoes, mixed vegetables, remaining rice and hot water. Cook, covered, for 20 minutes on medium. Serve garnished with hard-boiled eggs. Serves 4-6.

Microwave tip

• Layer prepared ingredients into a casserole dish as described above and microwave, covered, on Medium (50%) for 15 minutes to finish cooking the breyani.

AKHNI

500 ml rice
30 ml sunflower oil
1 large onion, thinly sliced
800 g mutton, cubed (preferably leg)
1 green chilli
10 ml salt
10 ml crushed fresh ginger
5 ml crushed garlic
5 ml ground jeera (cumin)
5 ml ground koljander (coriander)
5 ml ground barishap (fennel)
5 ml borrie (turmeric)
5 ml chilli powder
3 whole cloves
3 whole allspice
3 cardamom seeds
2 pieces stick cinnamon
1 tomato, grated or finely chopped
4 potatoes, halved
200 ml water
60 ml chopped green dhunia (coriander)
 leaves for decoration

Boil rice until just tender in salted water, about 20 minutes. Rinse and drain in a colander. Heat oil in a large saucepan and braise onions until golden, 5-10 minutes. Add meat and spices and cook, covered, over medium heat until meat is tender, 35-45 minutes. Add tomato, potatoes and water and cook until potatoes are nearly tender, about 15 minutes. Add rice, tossing with a fork to coat rice with gravy. Take care not to let rice get too mushy. Steam, tightly covered, over low heat for a further 20 minutes. Sprinkle dhunia leaves over just before serving with atjars and salads. Serves 8.

Note

• This is an easy way of serving curry and rice as these ingredients are cooked in one pot so that the rice becomes moist and takes on the flavour of the curry. It is a popular wedding dish.

Curries

MINCE CURRY WITH PEAS

500 g steak mince
30 ml oil
2 large onions, sliced
1 large tomato, grated or pulverized
10 ml crushed green ginger
5 ml crushed garlic
3 pieces stick cinnamon
5 cardamon seeds, slightly bruised
3 whole cloves
10 ml roasted masala
5 ml borrie (turmeric)
5 ml ground jeera (cumin)
5 ml ground koljander (coriander)
2 potatoes, peeled and quartered
250 ml frozen peas

Wash and drain mince. Heat oil and cook onions until transparent. Add tomatoes and cook a further 10 minutes. Add all the spices and simmer for about 15 minutes, or until well blended. Crumble mince into sauce, stirring. Cook covered, for 20 minutes, then add potatoes and cook until almost tender, about 15 minutes. Add frozen peas. Cook for further 10 minutes. Serve hot with roti, rice and sambals. Serve 4-6

Salomi: Fill a roti with about 50 ml mince curry mixture and roll up. It makes a delicious light supper or snack.

Mince curry with peas served with mixed vegetable atjar. A roti filled with mince curry is known as a Salomi, *a popular Malay take-away and TV snack.*

MALAY CURRY

Malay curries generally contain meat in some form or another and have less chilli and more spices, such as cardamom, barishap and jeera, than Indian curries. They are also slightly sweeter and are almost always eaten with rice or rotis and a selection of fresh salads or sambals, such as tomato and onion salad, cucumber sambal or green pepper salad. Dried fruit, jam or chutney are not usually added to Malay curries, which may be fairly dry like gheema curry or mince curry, or sauce-like as with dhal curry. If a thicker curry is required, more onion and tomato should be added. This way the full spicy flavour of the curry is retained. Sometimes potato is added for extra body.

Malay curries are considered a meal in themselves and are traditionally eaten with the fingers. From an early age Malay children learn to break off pieces of roti and wrap them around the rich curry mixture.

PENANG CURRY

Penang curry originated in Java. It is a fairly dry curry and does not have much sauce.

500 g mutton or lamb, cubed
30 ml sunflower oil
2 onions, thinly sliced
150 ml water

Marinade
3 cloves garlic, crushed
5 ml salt
3 ml borrie (turmeric)
8 ml curry powder
2 bay leaves
30 ml vinegar
45 ml sugar

Combine marinade ingredients and rub into meat. Set meat aside for about 1 hour. Heat oil in a saucepan and braise onions until golden, 5-10 minutes. Add marinated meat and water and cook for about 45 minutes, or until meat is tender. Serve with mashed potatoes and salads. Serves 4.

DHAL CURRY

Red lentil curry. The dhal adds liquid to the curry, which gives it a fair amount of gravy.

500 ml dhal (red lentils)
500 ml water
1 kg lamb or mutton, cubed
30 ml sunflower oil
2 large onions, thinly sliced
250 ml hot water

Marinade
10 ml crushed fresh ginger
5 ml crushed garlic
2 pieces stick cinnamon
3 cardamom seeds
3 whole cloves
5 ml borrie (turmeric)
10 ml roasted masala
30 ml tomato paste or 1 ripe tomato, chopped
2 ml sugar (optional)
100 ml water

Soak dhal in 500 ml water for 1 hour. Combine all marinade ingredients and marinate meat in mixture for 30 minutes. Heat oil in a large saucepan and braise onions until golden, 5-10 minutes. Add meat and marinade and cook for 30-40 minutes over medium heat, or until meat is tender. Add soaked dhal with hot water and cook a further 15-20 minutes, or until tender. (Dhal must be very soft and mushy.) Serve hot with white rice and salads. Serves 8-10.

Mutton curry served with golden-fried puris *(page 49), a variety of sambals and Kumquat atjar (page 62).*

MUTTON CURRY

This mutton curry has a thick, tasty gravy.

500 g mutton or lamb, cubed
5 ml crushed garlic
10 ml crushed fresh ginger
5 ml ground jeera (cumin)
5 ml ground koljander (coriander)
3 pieces stick cinnamon
3 cardamom seeds
4 whole cloves
5 ml borrie (turmeric)
5 ml chilli powder
5 ml salt
30 ml sunflower oil
2 large onions, thinly sliced
150 ml water
250 ml grated or finely chopped tomato
2 ml sugar (optional)
3 medium potatoes, halved
250 ml hot water
60 ml chopped green dhunia (coriander) leaves (optional)

Wash and drain meat in a colander. Combine with spices and salt. Heat oil in a large saucepan and braise onions for 5-10 minutes, or until golden brown. Add meat and 100 ml water and cook over medium heat until meat and spices are well-blended, about 30 minutes. Add tomato and sugar and cook a further 10 mintues, or until tomato is absorbed into gravy. Add potatoes and hot water and cook until potatoes are soft, about 15 minutes, adding more hot water if a thinner gravy is desired. Sprinkle with dhunia leaves and cook for 2 minutes before serving with Roti*, Puri* or white rice. Serves 4-6.

Variation
• Add 250 ml frozen or canned peas after adding potatoes.

GHEEMA CURRY

A traditional curry made with cubed beef steak called 'gheema'.

15 ml sunflower oil
2 large onions, very thinly sliced
5 cardamom seeds
5 whole cloves
4 pieces stick cinnamon, each 2 cm long
2 tomatoes, chopped
10 ml salt
4 cloves garlic
small piece green ginger
1 kg gheema (cubed steak), washed and drained well
5 ml borrie (turmeric)
10 ml red leaf masala
5 ml ground koljander (coriander)
5 ml ground jeera (cumin)
3 large potatoes, quartered
2 ml sugar

Combine oil, onions, cardamom seeds, cloves and cinnamon in a large saucepan.

Braise the onions until lightly browned, about 5-10 minutes, then add chopped tomato, and salt, garlic and ginger pounded together in a mortar and pestle. Simmer for about 8-10 minutes. Add gheema and simmer for 15 minutes. Add borrie, masala, koljander and jeera and simmer for 15 minutes. If mixture is too dry, add 200 ml water. Add potatoes and sugar and simmer until potatoes are cooked, about 15 minutes. Serves 10.

Variations

• Add 6 hard-boiled eggs, quartered, instead of potatoes.
• Add 1 x 410 g can peas, drained, or 400 g frozen peas just after adding the potatoes.

FRIKKADEL CURRY

For a thicker curry with a tangier taste, stir approximately 250 ml natural yoghurt into the mixture after the frikkadels have cooked for 15 minutes.

30 ml sunflower oil
2 large onions, thinly sliced
250 ml grated or very finely chopped
    tomato
2 ml borrie (turmeric)
2 ml salt
5 ml crushed garlic
1 green chilli, halved
2 bay leaves
5 ml ground jeera (cumin)
5 ml ground koljander (coriander)
10 ml roasted masala
100 ml water

Frikkadels
600 g steak mince
2 ml freshly ground white pepper
5 ml salt
5 ml crushed garlic
2 ml ground cinnamon
2 ml ground nutmeg
1 egg

Combine ingredients for frikkadels and form into balls. Heat oil in a large saucepan and braise the onions until golden, 5-10 minutes. Add tomato and remaining ingredients and cook, covered, over medium heat until well-blended, about 15 minutes, stirring occasionally. Add frikkadels and cook a further 20-25 minutes. Serve hot with white rice. Serves 6.

Sugar bean curry served with Malay rotis.

SUGAR BEAN CURRY

300 g sugar beans, soaked overnight in
    water to cover
20 ml sunflower oil
1 large onion, thinly sliced
500 g mutton or lamb, cubed
200 ml water
1 green chilli, chopped
10 ml crushed garlic
10 ml crushed fresh ginger
3 cardamom seeds
3 pieces stick cinnamon
5 ml borrie (turmeric)
10 ml red leaf masala
1 large tomato, grated or finely chopped
5 ml salt, or to taste
5 ml sugar, or to taste (optional)

Drain sugar beans and cook in water to cover until farily soft, about 1 hour. Meanwhile heat oil in a large saucepan and braise onions until golden, 5-10 minutes. Add well-washed and drained meat, water, spices and tomato and cook for about 30 minutes or until meat is nearly tender. Add sugar beans and cook them until well-blended, about 15 minutes. Add salt and sugar to taste. Serve with Roti* or white rice and atjars. Serves 6.

Microwave tip

• Add 800 ml hot water to soaked and drained beans and microwave, covered, for 10 minutes on Full Power (100%) then a further 30-40 minutes on Medium High (70%). The beans must be tender but still whole. Continue as described above.

Puris, Rotis and Rice

MALAY ROTIS

These are lighter and softer in texture than Indian rotis, and richer in flavour because they are fried in oil. A roti rolled around a mince curry filling is known as a Salomi (page 45).

750 ml cake flour
100 ml self-raising flour
5 ml salt
45 ml sunflower oil or softened butter
250 ml cold water
100 ml butter
100 ml flour
50 ml melted butter mixed with 50 ml
sunflower oil

Combine flour, self-raising flour and salt in a bowl. Add oil or butter, rubbing it into flour to form a crumbly mixture. Add water and mix to a soft dough. Knead, adding extra flour to make an even-textured, pliable dough. Leave to rest for 30 minutes, covered. Divide dough into 7-8 pieces. Roll each out on a very lightly floured surface to a circle 20 cm in diameter, dot with 15 ml butter and sprinkle with flour. Roll and stretch into thick ropes of dough (Fig. 1). Roll up both ends of the ropes; one side clockwise, one anti-clockwise (2), and fold one half flat on top of the other (3). Rotis may be frozen at this stage, interleaved with plastic. Allow to rest for about 1 hour, covered. Roll out on a lightly floured surface to circles about 20 cm in diameter. Heat a heavy-based frying pan and fry rotis one at a time, turning occasionally and brushing with melted butter and oil mixture (about 10 ml in all for each one). Fry until golden brown and lightly speckled. Remove from pan and pat between your palms to fluff surface. Serve hot with curries. Makes 7-8.

Microwave tip
• To reheat rotis, microwave, covered, on Medium (50%) for 20-30 seconds per roti.

Flaky Malay rotis (top left) and Indian rotis (bottom right); Puris (top right) are lightly browned and puffed up.

ROTI

A roti is unleavened bread made either from cake flour or bread flour and maize meal and is served instead of rice with curry. It originated in India, but like so many Indian dishes it has been adopted by, and adapted to suit, the Cape Malays' taste. Rotis are cooked on a tava — a special frying pan without handles — until lightly flecked and golden brown. A heavy-based frying pan may also be used. The Indian community uses ghee (clarified butter) rather than melted butter to make rotis. To eat roti, break off a piece with your fingers and wrap it around a little curry. Generally, using knives and forks is out of place when eating curry with roti.

To make ghee: Boil butter until quite clear, skimming off scum every time it foams. Strain through muslin to remove all impurities and store resulting clear liquid in an enamel or glass jar in the refrigerator. Use as required.

INDIAN ROTIS

A soft flat bread similar to pita bread.

200 ml boiling water
30 ml malai or milk
65 ml white maize meal
75 ghee or softened butter
500 ml cake flour
2 ml salt
60 ml ghee or melted butter
100 ml flour

Pour water and malai over maize meal. Cool slightly. Add ghee or butter and mix well. Add sifted flour and salt and knead to a soft, even-textured dough. Cover with a cloth or plastic and set aside for about 1 hour. Divide dough into 5 pieces and roll each out to about 20 cm in diameter. Brush with ghee or melted butter and sprinkle with flour. Fold in half, brush top with more ghee

and sprinkle with more flour. Fold in half again (to make quarters). Set aside, covered, for 30 minutes. Sprinkle a board lightly with flour and roll each roti out to about 20 cm in diameter. Fry each in a heated frying pan, turning several times and brushing frequently with ghee, until speckled and golden brown. Serve hot. Serves 5.

Note
• Malai is the thick cream that forms on top of boiled full-cream milk.

1

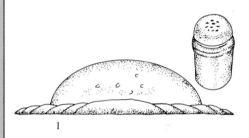
2

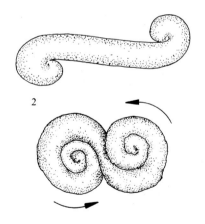
3

INDIAN PURIS

Puris are very light and puff up when they come into contact with hot oil. Although generally served as bread with vegetable or lentil curries, they are also very good spread lightly with butter and topped with jam.

500 ml cake flour
2 ml salt
175 ml ghee or melted butter
100 ml warm milk
100 ml water
500 ml sunflower oil

Sift flour and salt. Rub ghee or butter into flour with your fingertips until crumbly. Combine milk and water, add to flour mixture and mix to a soft dough. Moisten hands with a little oil and knead dough until smooth and elastic. Break off small pieces of dough the size of ping-pong balls and roll out on a lightly floured surface into circles about 7 cm in diameter. Heat oil until fairly hot and deep-fry puris, 2 or 3 at a time, until puffed and golden brown on both sides, about 1 minute. Press puris into oil with a slotted spoon to ensure that they puff up. Remove from oil and drain on absorbent paper. Serve hot or cold. Makes about 18-20.

Note
• Drained and cooled puris keep well in an airtight container for up to 1 week.

ALMOND YELLOW RICE

500 ml water
250 ml uncooked long-grain rice
2 pieces stick cinnamon
4 cardamom seeds
2 ml borrie (turmeric)
5 ml salt
50 g blanched almonds
50 ml sugar
50 ml butter or margarine

Bring water to boil. Add rice, cinnamon, cardamom seeds, borrie and salt and cook, uncovered, until quite soft, about 20 minutes. Drain in a colander and rinse with cold water. Return rice to saucepan with almonds and sugar and dot with butter or margarine. Steam, covered, over medium heat for about 10 minutes, turning lightly every now and then. Serves 6.

Yellow rice with raisins: Add 100 ml raisins, currants or sultanas instead of almonds.

Coconut yellow rice: Add 100 ml desiccated coconut instead of almonds.

Microwave tip
• For a fluffier rice, microwave on Medium (50%) for about 5 minutes instead of steaming.

DHAL RICE

Chana dhal, also known as Durban dhal, is the Indian term for yellow split peas. To cut down on cooking time, first soak dhal in water to cover for about 1 hour.

500 ml uncooked rice
water
15 ml salt
2 pieces stick cinnamon
3 cloves
125 ml chana dhal (yellow split peas)
2 ml ground jeera (cumin)
50 ml butter
150 ml water

Boil rice in plenty of water with salt, cinnamon and cloves until tender, about 20 minutes. Boil chana dhal separately in water to cover until quite soft, about 25 minutes. Drain and rinse rice and chana dhal. Combine in a saucepan, add jeera and dot with butter. Sprinkle water over and steam on medium heat for 10-15 minutes. Serves 6.

Microwave tip
• Microwave uncooked rice and precooked chana dhal on Full Power (100%) for 5 minutes, then for 15 minutes on Medium (50%). Drain and rinse, then place in a casserole dish, add jeera and dot with butter. Sprinkle water over and microwave on Medium (50%) for 10 minutes.

PRAWN RICE

An unusual rice dish baked in the oven.

50 ml sunflower oil
100 g butter
1 large onion, thinly sliced
5 ml crushed garlic
2 pieces stick cinnamon
3 cardamom seeds
1 large tomato, thinly sliced
5 ml salt
5 ml chilli powder
1 green pepper, seeded and diced
500 g rice
salted water
450 g prawns, shelled and deveined

Heat oil and 50 g butter. Add onion, garlic, cinnamon and cardamom seeds and braise until onions are golden, 5-10 minutes. Add tomato, salt and chilli powder and cook a further 10 minutes. Add green pepper and cook a further 5 minutes. Meanwhile, parboil rice in salted water to cover for 15 minutes. Melt remaining butter in a frying pan and cook prawns until pink, about 5-10 minutes. Combine all ingredients in a casserole dish and bake in the oven at 180 °C for 20-30 minutes. Serve with Masala fish*. Serves 6-8.

Microwave tip
• Microwave finished dish on Medium (50%) for 12-15 minutes instead of baking in the oven.

GESMOORDE RYS

500 ml uncooked long-grain rice
1 onion, thinly sliced
50 ml butter or margarine
2 pieces stick cinnamon
4 cardamom seeds
2 cloves
10 ml salt
750 ml water

Wash rice until rinsing water is quite clear. Braise onion in butter or margarine until golden brown. Add spices and rice to onion, sprinkle salt and water over and steam, covered, over medium heat for 40-45 minutes, occasionally tossing rice with a fork. Serves 6-8.

Microwave tip
• Cook dish, covered, in the microwave on Medium (50%) for about 15 minutes instead of steaming.

Clockwise: *Savoury rice, Gesmoorde rys and Prawn rice.*

SAVOURY RICE

30 ml sunflower oil
30 ml butter
1 large onion, thinly sliced
1 green pepper, seeded and chopped
1 tomato, chopped
5 ml chilli powder or crushed dried red
   chillis
10 ml methi masala
5 ml salt
500 ml mixed frozen vegetables
500 ml long grain rice
60 ml butter

Heat oil and butter in a large saucepan and braise onion until golden, 5-10 minutes. Reserve a third of the onion for garnish. Add green pepper and tomato to saucepan with chilli powder, methi masala and salt and simmer for 15 minutes. Add frozen vegetables and simmer for 10 minutes. Meanwhile, parboil rice for 15 minutes in lightly salted water. Rinse, drain and add to saucepan with vegetables. Dot with butter and add reserved braised onion. Steam, covered, over medium heat for 15 minutes. Serves 6-8.

Vegetables, Salads and Sambals

GLAZED CARROTS WITH ALMONDS

500 g carrots
45 ml butter or margarine
45 ml brown sugar
2 ml salt
pinch chilli powder
50 ml water
50 g slivered blanched almonds
2 ml ground cinnamon

Peel carrots, then slice into long thin strips. Melt butter or margarine in a saucepan over medium heat and stir in sugar, salt, chilli powder and water. Add carrot strips and stir to coat completely. Reduce heat to low and simmer, covered, until carrots are tender, about 12 minutes. Add almonds and cook a further 5 minutes. Serve sprinkled with ground cinnamon. Serves 4-6.

Microwave tip
• Microwave butter or margarine, sugar, salt, chilli powder and 30 ml water on Full Power (100%) for 1½-2 minutes. Stir to blend. Add carrots and stir until coated. Microwave, covered, on Full Power (100%) for 6-8 minutes, stirring once. Add almonds and cook a further 1 minute. Sprinkle with ground cinnamon and serve.

ORANGE-BAKED PUMPKIN

500 g pumpkin, cut into chunks
125 g dried peaches or apricots
125 ml fresh orange juice
5 ml brown sugar
1 piece stick cinnamon
15 ml butter

Place pumpkin and peaches or apricots in an oven bag. Cover pumpkin with orange juice, sprinkle sugar over and add cinnamon stick. Dot with butter and secure bag, piercing a hole near the top to allow the steam to escape. Place in an ovenproof dish and bake at 180 °C for 30 minutes, or until pumpkin is tender. Serves 4.

SMOOR TOMATO AND ONION

A tasty versatile sauce. For a quick meal add chopped cold meats, sausage or tuna and serve on toast or with rice. This sauce also makes the ideal base for a pizza.

30 ml sunflower oil
1 large onion, thinly sliced
2 large ripe tomatoes, chopped
1 green chilli, chopped
15 ml sugar, or to taste
salt to taste

Heat oil in a saucepan and braise onion until golden, 5-10 minutes. Add tomatoes and chilli and cook for 15 minutes over medium heat, or until well-combined. Add sugar and salt to taste and serve hot with Fish frikkadels*. Serves 4.

FRIED POTATOES

50 ml sunflower oil
1 large onion, thinly sliced
3 large potatoes
5 ml salt
10 ml crushed jeera (cumin)
30 ml water

Heat oil in a large frying pan and fry onion until golden, 5-10 minutes. Slice potatoes in circles 5 mm thick, add to onions and sprinkle with salt and jeera. Add water and cook, covered, over medium heat for 10 minutes, or until potatoes are tender, stirring occasionally. Serve hot. Serves 4.

Variation
• Slice potatoes thickly and soak in salted water. Meanwhile, whisk 1 egg with 2 ml salt and 2 ml chilli powder. Drain potatoes well, dip them in egg mixture, then coat lightly in flour. Shallow-fry in hot oil until golden, 10-15 minutes. Drain and serve with Masala fish* and Fried brinjals in batter*.

VEGETABLE CURRY

Any fresh vegetables may be used in this curry.

100 ml sunflower oil
6 small potatoes, peeled
30 ml butter
2 large onions, thinly sliced
2 tomatoes, chopped or puréed
10 ml crushed ginger
5 ml crushed garlic
2 whole green chillis
5 ml chilli powder
5 ml borrie (turmeric)
10 ml ground jeera (cumin)
5 ml ground koljander (coriander)
1,5-2 kg mixed fresh cabbage, carrots, peas
   and cauliflower
salt to taste

Heat oil in a large deep saucepan and fry whole potatoes over high heat until golden, about 5 minutes. Drain potatoes and set aside. Add butter to oil in saucepan and braise onions until golden, 5-10 minutes. Add tomatoes, ginger, garlic and chillis and simmer, covered, over medium heat for 15 minutes. Add spices and simmer, covered, until well-blended, about 10 minutes. Cut carrots into thin strips, shred cabbage and break cauliflower into florets. Add to curry with peas and potatoes. Simmer, covered, until the vegetables are tender, about 20 minutes. Season to taste with salt. Serve hot with white rice. Serves 8.

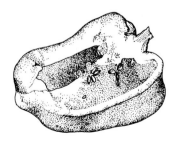

From top to bottom: *Smoored brinjals and carrots, and Fried brinjals in batter.*

Dip brinjal slices in batter and fry for 5-8 minutes on each side, or until crisp and golden. Drain on absorbent paper and serve hot with Masala fish*. Serves 4.

YELLOW SPLIT PEA CURRY

Yellow split peas are usually referred to as Durban dhal. This vegetarian curry is more like a sauce and is the perfect accompaniment to Masala fish*.

500 g yellow split peas
1 litre water
60 ml butter
3 large onions, thinly sliced
250 ml grated or very finely chopped
    tomato
5 ml sugar
2 pieces stick cinnamon
3 cardamom seeds
5 ml chilli powder
10 ml crushed fresh ginger
5 ml crushed garlic
10 ml ground jeera (cumin)
10 ml ground koljander (coriander)
2 ml borrie (turmeric)
a few curry leaves
60 ml chopped green dhunia (coriander)

Boil peas in water until very soft, about 35-45 minutes. Remove from heat and purée in a food processor or blender, or rub through a sieve. Melt butter in a large saucepan and braise onions until golden, 5-10 minutes. Reserve a third. Add tomato, sugar, cinnamon, cardamom seeds, chilli, ginger, garlic, jeera, koljander and borrie to saucepan and cook over medium heat until well-blended, about 15 minutes. Add cooked peas and cook a further 10 minutes. Remove from heat and add curry leaves, dhunia and reserved onions just before serving with Gesmoorde rice* and atjars. Serves 8.

SMOORED BRINJALS AND CARROTS

10 ml butter
10 ml sunflower oil
1 onion, thinly sliced
1 green chilli, finely chopped
5 ml ground koljander (coriander)
5 ml ground jeera (cumin)
2 carrots, coarsely grated
1 brinjal, cubed
250 ml frozen peas
salt to taste

Heat butter and oil in a saucepan, add onion and braise until golden, 5-10 minutes. Add chilli, koljander and jeera and simmer for 5 minutes. Add carrots, brinjal and peas and cook for 15 minutes, or until vegetables are tender. Season to taste with salt and serve with any fish dish. Serves 4-6.

FRIED BRINJALS IN BATTER

3 large brinjals
2 ml salt
100 ml sunflower oil

Batter
250 ml cake flour
250 ml self-raising flour
5 ml salt
5 ml ground jeera (cumin)
5 ml ground koljander (coriander)
5 ml chilli powder
15 ml sunflower oil
375 ml water

Wash and slice brinjals, leaving skin on. Sprinkle with salt and set aside for 15 minutes. Rinse under cold water and pat dry. *Batter:* Combine all ingredients to make a soft batter. Heat oil in a large frying pan.

Gesmoorde kool (braised cabbage) and Gebraaide patats (baked sweet potatoes).

GESMOORDE KOOL

Braised cabbage is a traditional Malay dish usually served with fish.

30 ml sunflower oil
2 onions, thinly sliced
10 ml sugar
2 ml crushed dried chillis
5 ml crushed garlic
1 small cabbage, finely shredded
salt to taste

Heat the oil in a large saucepan and braise onions until quite brown, about 10 minutes. Add sugar, chillis and garlic and cook for 5 minutes, stirring. Add cabbage and cook, stirring occasionally, until lightly browned, 10-15 minutes. Add salt to taste and serve. Serves 4-6.

MASHED POTATOES

600 g potatoes, peeled and quartered
150 ml water
2 ml salt
45 ml butter
125 ml hot milk
5 ml baking powder
2 ml ground nutmeg for garnish
10 ml chopped parsley for garnish

Cook potatoes, covered, in salted water until tender, 15-20 minutes. Drain. Add butter and hot milk and mash to a fine smooth consistency. Add baking powder and beat until fluffy. Serve garnished with nutmeg and parsley, as an accompaniment to Sosatie chops* or Frikkadels with smoor tomato and onion*. Serves 4.

GEBRAAIDE PATATS

The name *borrie patat* comes from the yellow colour of the flesh of this particular variety of sweet potato, considered to be one of the tastiest. The following is a simple recipe for baked sweet potatoes.

1 kg borrie patats (sweet potatoes)

Wash sweet potatoes very well and pat dry. Place on a baking sheet and bake at 180 °C for 35-45 minutes, or until insides are soft. To test if sweet potatoes are done, squeeze them lightly. The flesh should give and the skin should be crisp. Serve with braaied meats and salads. Serves 4.

Salads & Sambals

TOMATO AND ONION SALAD

Chopped dhunia leaves make an excellent garnish for this salad.

1 large onion, very thinly sliced
5 ml salt
500 ml hot water
2 large ripe tomatoes, chopped
5 ml crushed dried red chillis
10 ml sugar
30 ml white vinegar

Sprinkle onion with salt, and rub it in well. Pour hot water over and leave to drain in a colander. Squeeze out excess moisture. Combine onion with remaining ingredients. Serves 4-6.

Cucumber and onion salad: Use 1 large English cucumber, peeled and sliced, or 2 ordinary ones, instead of tomato. Scrape peeled cucumber with the tines of a fork before slicing, for a decorative edge.

TUNA SALAD

This salad can also be served on toast for Sunday supper.

1 onion, thinly sliced
salt
500 ml boiling water
1 small green pepper, seeded and chopped
1 firm ripe tomato, chopped
1 x 200 g can shredded tuna
2 ml chilli powder
60 ml mayonnaise or salad cream
lettuce leaves

Sprinkle onion with salt, pour boiling water over and drain well in a colander, squeezing out all excess moisture. Combine with green pepper, tomato and tuna and sprinkle with chilli powder. Add mayonnaise or salad cream and combine well. Serve on lettuce leaves. Serves 4-6.

BEETROOT AND ONION SALAD

Sprinkle a little coarsely ground black pepper over just before serving. For variation, grate beetroot and chop onions finely, then sprinkle with 50 ml vinegar.

4 large or 6 medium beetroot
2 medium onions, cut into rings
10 ml salt
500 ml hot water
250 ml brown vinegar
10 ml sugar

Boil beetroot in water to cover until very tender, about 45 minutes. (They are ready if they give when pierced with a fork.) Peel and slice beetroot thinly. Sprinkle onions with salt, pour boiling water over and drain onions very well in a colander. Combine beetroot and onions, pour vinegar over and sprinkle with sugar and extra salt. Serve with Kebaabs* and Almond yellow rice*. Serves 6-8.

Cook's tip
• Beetroot may be cooked in a pressure cooker to save time; it will take 15-20 minutes at 100 kPa.

PINEAPPLE AND CARROT SALAD

Serve this salad with rich spicy foods like breyani. For variation, shred a few lettuce leaves and add to salad.

1 pineapple
3 carrots
1 onion
salt
500 ml hot water
1 green pepper, seeded and cubed
20 ml white vinegar
10 ml sugar

Peel and grate pineapple and carrots coarsely. Chop onions very finely and sprinkle with salt. Pour hot water over and drain very well in a colander, squeezing out excess moisture. Combine pineapple, carrots and onion with green pepper in a bowl, and stir in vinegar, sugar and a little extra salt. Serves 6.

MIXED FRUIT AND VEGETABLE SALAD

For variation, toss salad with 50 ml salad cream just before serving and add 50 ml chopped mixed nuts.

1 medium pineapple, peeled and coarsely chopped
1 red apple, cored and chopped
1 Granny Smith apple, cored and chopped
2 carrots, grated
60 ml seedless raisins
1 small English cucumber, thinly sliced
1 green pepper, seeded and cubed
a few lettuce leaves, shredded
1 avocado pear, peeled, stoned and sliced for garnish
a little lemon juice

Combine pineapple, apples, carrots, raisins, cucumber, green pepper and lettuce leaves in a salad bowl. Garnish with avocado pear slices, sprinkled with lemon juice to prevent discolouring. Serves 8.

DATE SALAD

Dates are one of the most important gifts brought home by pilgrims from Mecca. These dates are not quite as sweet as the ones obtainable here and are larger in size.

1 large onion, thinly sliced
salt
500 ml boiling water
500 g stoned fresh dates
5 ml crushed dried red chillis
10 ml sugar
150 ml brown vinegar

Sprinkle onion with salt, pour boiling water over and drain well in a colander, squeezing out excess moisture. Quarter dates and layer in a bowl with onions, sprinkling each layer with crushed chillis. Dissolve sugar in vinegar and pour over dates and onions. Serves 6-8.

Mixed fruit and vegetable salad, and Date salad, which is reserved for special occasions.

The 'bite' in this Carrot sambal comes from both green and red chilli peppers.

KWEPER SAMBAL

This recipe for quince sambal is very traditional. However the chopped dhunia leaves may be omitted if desired.

1 large quince
5 ml salt
5 ml crushed garlic
5 ml crushed green chilli
30 ml lemon juice or white vinegar
50 ml chopped green dhunia (coriander)
leaves

Peel and grate quince. Sprinkle with salt and allow to draw for 15 minutes. Squeeze out all moisture and combine quince with remaining ingredients. Serve with fish or bredies. Makes about 250 ml.

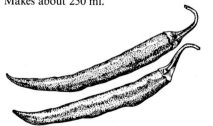

CUCUMBER SAMBAL

English cucumbers make excellent sambals as they are seldom bitter.

1 large English cucumber
5 ml salt
5 ml crushed garlic
5 ml crushed green chilli or 1 green chilli,
chopped
30 ml white vinegar
5 ml sugar (optional)

Peel and grate cucumber, sprinkle with salt and allow to draw for 15 minutes. Squeeze out all moisture and combine cucumber with remaining ingredients. Serve with hot curries. Makes about 250 ml.

WORTEL SAMBAL

If you like, garnish this carrot sambal with a handful of plumped-up seedless raisins or sultanas.

5 carrots
5 ml salt
1 small onion, finely grated
5 ml crushed garlic
1 green chilli, finely chopped
30 ml lemon juice or white vinegar
5 ml sugar, or to taste

Peel and coarsely grate carrots. Sprinkle with salt and allow to draw for 15 minutes. Drain off moisture and combine carrot with remaining ingredients. Makes about 250 ml.

SAMBALS

The word 'sambal' is Javanese in origin and means condiment. It is usually a highly seasoned relish of grated raw fruits or vegetables, squeezed dry, mixed with pounded chilli and moistened with vinegar or lemon juice for a sweet-sour taste. Sambals are usually served with a fragrant curry or bredie. Today dhunia and garlic are also added for extra flavour.

APPLE SAMBAL

Serve this fresh-tasting sambal with bredie.

3 large Granny Smith apples
5 ml salt
1 green chilli, finely chopped
15 ml lemon juice or white vinegar
10 ml sugar, or to taste

Peel, core and grate apples coarsely, sprinkle with salt and allow to draw for 15 minutes. Squeeze out moisture (apple should be fairly dry). Add remaining ingredients and mix well. Makes about 350 ml.

AVOCADO PEAR SAMBAL

This unusual sambal has a smooth texture and a slightly tangy flavour.

1 large ripe avocado pear, peeled, stoned
    and mashed
250 ml natural yoghurt
4 green chillis
½ small bunch green dhunia (coriander)
    leaves
10 ml sugar

Combine avocado pear and yoghurt. Grind chillis and dhunia leaves in a blender or food processor, then mix into avocado mixture. Stir in sugar. Makes about 350 ml.

PINEAPPLE SAMBAL

Delicious with a rich-tasting bredie or curry.

1 medium pineapple
4 green chillis
1 small bunch green dhunia (coriander)
    leaves
10 ml sugar
10 ml whole jeera (cumin) seeds

Peel and grate pineapple. Grind chillis and dhunia leaves in a blender or food processor and mix with pineapple and sugar. Sprinkle jeera seeds over. Makes about 500 ml.

A variety of sambals to serve with curry.
Clockwise: *Pineapple, Avocado pear and Apple sambal.*

Blatjang, Atjars and Konfyt

DRIED RED CHILLI BLATJANG

A traditional Malay blatjang which is a type of chilli sauce. I remember having to painstakingly pound dry red chillis in a mortar and pestle every Monday. Mondays were generally fish days in District Six, and fish served without blatjang just didn't seem right.

60 ml smooth apricot jam
250 ml brown vinegar
100 g crushed dried red chillis
10 ml crushed garlic
2 ml salt

Mix jam and vinegar to a smooth paste. Add remaining ingredients and mix until well-blended. Serve with Fish frikkadels* or other fish dishes. This blatjang will keep almost indefinitely in an airtight container. Makes about 400 ml.

DHUNIA BLATJANG

This is similar to the traditional red chilli blatjang. It is Indian in origin, hence hot and spicy. Add 30 ml chopped mint leaves for variation.

1 bunch green dhunia (coriander), stems
    removed
2 green peppers, seeded and chopped
2 whole green chillis
3 cloves garlic
1 tomato, chopped
2 ml salt
60 ml fresh lemon juice
2 ml crushed jeera (cumin) seeds

Combine all ingredients in a blender or food processor and purée until smooth. Serve with roasts or meat dishes.
Makes about 300 ml.

Clockwise: Lemon atjar, Dried fruit blatjang, Mixed vegetable atjar, Dried red chilli blatjang. Centre: *Dhunia blatjang.*

DRIED FRUIT BLATJANG

A thick fruity chutney.

200 g dried peaches
250 g dried apricots
500 ml water
1 onion, grated
50 ml crushed dried red chillis
10 ml crushed garlic
400 ml brown vinegar
350 ml sugar
5 ml salt, or to taste

Wash dried fruit well and soak in water until soft. Simmer in the same water until soft and mushy, 30-45 minutes. Combine grated onion, chilli and garlic and add to fruit. Heat vinegar and dissolve sugar in it. Add fruit mixture and simmer until smooth. Add salt. Cool before bottling in sterilised jars. Serve with fish or use in a meat marinade. Makes about 1 kg.

Cook's tip
• For an even smoother texture, purée blatjang in a blender or food processor once cooled.

EASY LEMON ATJAR

1 kg fresh lemons
75 ml salt
750 ml white vinegar
150 ml sunflower oil
25 ml chilli powder
5 ml crushed koljander (coriander) seeds
5 ml crushed jeera (cumin) seeds
100 ml methi masala
65 ml sugar
5 ml mustard powder

Wash lemons well and dry. Cut each into eighths and remove pips. Dissolve salt in vinegar and soak lemons in it for 48 hours, stirring often to ensure that all lemons are well-soaked. Pour off excess liquid. Add remaining ingredients and mix well. Bottle in sterilised jars and seal. Use after 24 hours. Makes 1 kg.

MIXED VEGETABLE ATJAR

10 ml bicarbonate of soda
6 large carrots, peeled and cut into thin
    strips
1 small cauliflower, broken into florets
1 large onion, finely sliced
½ green cabbage, finely sliced
250 ml fresh or frozen peas
50 ml atjar masala
5 ml salt
5 cloves garlic, crushed
400 ml cooking oil

To a large saucepan of boiling water, add bicarbonate of soda and steep prepared vegetables in it for about 2 minutes. Drain well, then cover with cold water immediately. Drain again and allow vegetables to dry in a sunny place for about 10 hours. Mix atjar masala, salt and garlic with 30 ml cooking oil to form a paste. Heat remaining cooking oil and add the atjar masala mixture. Pour over vegetables and toss to mix, making sure vegetables are well coated. Place in a covered container in the refrigerator or pack in smaller sterilised jars and seal well. Store in a cool, dark place. This atjar can be eaten immediately, but is best after 2-3 weeks. Makes about 3 litres.

BLATJANG AND ATJAR

Malay blatjang is essentially a tangy chilli sauce, the main characteristic of which gives it its name, for example red chilli blatjang and dhunia blatjang. This traditional blatjang should not be confused with ordinary chutney.

Atjar is another favourite relish or pickle. It is made from sliced vegetables or fruits mixed with a special blend of spices, then packed in jars and covered with vinegar or oil.

KUMQUAT ATJAR

The perfect way to make use of this unusual citrus fruit. Lemons, cut into eighths, may be used instead of kumquats.

2 kg kumquats
250 g salt
200 g atjar masala
50 g chilli powder
50 ml crushed garlic
1 x 50 g can English mustard powder
**   mixed with 250 ml white vinegar**
1½ x 750 ml bottles sunflower oil

Halve kumquats and remove seeds. Place in a large flat dish and sprinkle salt over. Soak for 48 hours, then drain and dry in sun for a day. Add atjar masala, chilli powder, garlic, mustard and vinegar and spoon into sterilised jars. Bring oil to boil and pour over kumquats to cover. Use immediately, or seal and store for later use. Makes 2 kg.

Brinjal atjar: Parboil 2 kg cubed brinjals in lightly salted water for 5 minutes. Drain well and sun dry for 1 day. Add atjar masala, chilli powder, garlic, 10 ml salt and mustard powder mixed with vinegar in which 45 ml sugar has been dissolved. Spoon into sterilised jars. Bring oil to boil and pour over brinjals to cover. Store in a cool, dark place for at least a week before using.

GREEN MANGO ATJAR

1 kg green mangoes
10 ml salt, or to taste
250 ml sunflower oil
45 ml atjar masala
5 ml mustard powder
6 green chillis, crushed
3 green chillis, halved
20 ml crushed garlic
200 ml white vinegar

Wash mangoes well, leave skin on and cut into 2 cm chunks, discarding pips. Add remaining ingredients and mix well. Place in a large container, cover and leave for 3 days, tossing and stirring often. Use immediately, or bottle and seal for later use. Makes 1 kg.

Kumquat atjar and Green mango atjar.

Dried apricot konfyt and Green fig preserve.

DRIED APRICOT KONFYT

Konfyts are usually served on their own as a sweet at weddings and feasts.

750 g dried apricots
500 ml water
500 ml sugar
3 whole cloves
2 pieces stick cinnamon

Soak apricots in water for 1 hour, then transfer (with water) to a heavy-based saucepan. Sprinkle sugar over and add spices. Cook over low heat for 1 hour, stirring occasionally. Apricots must be tender and syrup thick. Bottle immediately in sterilised jars. May be used immediately or stored, tightly sealed, for later use. Makes 750 g.

GREEN FIG PRESERVE

My grandmother always said one should not pick green figs for preserving after the end of October, as the first crop then starts to ripen and will be bitter if preserved.

2 kg green figs (from first crop)
2,5 kg sugar
2,5 litres water
2 ml lemon juice
5 ml ground dried ginger

Lime solution
5 litres water
25 ml slaked lime
5 ml bicarbonate of soda

Scrape figs with a fine grater or a serrated knife to remove some skin and cut a cross in stem end of each. Combine ingredients for lime solution and soak figs in it overnight. Rinse well and drain. Bring about 3 litres water to boil, add figs and boil until tender, about 20 minutes. Drain. Bring sugar, water, lemon juice and ginger to boil. Add figs one by one and boil rapidly until figs are tender yet crisp and syrup is thick, 45 minutes-1 hour. Bottle in hot sterilised jars, pouring syrup over to cover. Seal. Makes 2 kg.

Glacé figs: Boil figs in syrup for about 30 minutes longer. Remove figs from syrup and drain on a wire rack to crystallise, about 6 hours. Pack in airtight containers. Glacé figs may also be frozen, wrapped in plastic, until needed.

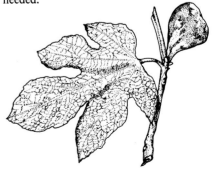

SOUR FIG PRESERVE

The wrinkled brown fruits of the Hottentot fig are available almost all year round but are at their best in late summer and autumn. Though sourish and slightly salty, the figs make an excellent jam or preserve. Use them before they are too dry and shrivelled; the skin should still be soft enough to remove easily after soaking. My granny used to skin the whole fig but nowadays we only take off the stem and trim the bottom.

1 kg sour figs
lightly salted water
750 g sugar
750 ml water
3 pieces stick cinnamon

Remove stalks and all loose leaves from figs and wash thoroughly. Soak overnight in lightly salted water to cover. Drain, then wash under cold running water and drain well. Remove skin if desired. In a heavy-based saucepan boil sugar, water and cinnamon until a thick syrup forms. Add figs and cook over medium heat until figs are tender but still whole, 1½-2 hours, stirring occasionally. Pour into hot sterilised jars. Use immediately or store, sealed. Makes 1 kg.

WATERMELON KONFYT

Either a preserving watermelon or an ordinary watermelon with a thick skin may be used. Remove thick outer skin and inner fleshy part, and use only the white peel just beneath the skin.

2 kg watermelon peel
lightly salted water
2 kg sugar
4 litres water
2 small pieces dried ginger
3 pieces stick cinnamon
20 ml lemon juice

Lime solution
5 litres water
30 ml slaked lime
5 ml bicarbonate of soda

Prick watermelon peel well on both sides with a fork and cut into even-sized squares. Combine ingredients for lime solution and soak peel in it overnight, covering with a plate or board to keep peel submerged. Drain, wash peel very well and leave in lightly salted water to cover for 1 hour. Boil in same water until just tender, about 30 minutes; peel should be able to be pierced easily with a match. Drain. Bring sugar, water, ginger, cinnamon and lemon juice to boil. Drop in peel, piece by piece, and boil over medium heat until peel is transparent and syrup is thick, about 2 hours. Pack in hot sterilised jars, pouring syrup over to cover, and seal immediately. Makes 2 kg.

Note
• Watermelon konfyt also keeps well if left to drain on wire racks until crystallised and packed away dry like glacé figs. Watermelon konfyt may also be frozen, wrapped in plastic, until needed.

CARROT AND PINEAPPLE KONFYT

A traditional konfyt served at weddings and festivals.

1 large bunch carrots
2 pineapples
800 g sugar
1 litre water
few pieces stick cinnamon
1 piece dried ginger
5 whole cloves

Scrape carrots clean and slice into thin rings, about 1 mm thick. Peel pineapple, slice and cut into chunks. Soak carrot and pineapple separately in lightly salted water overnight. Drain and steam together in very little water in saucepan until carrots are tender, about 10 minutes. Dissolve sugar in water and bring to the boil, stirring. Pour syrup over pineapple and carrots, add spices and simmer slowly until the syrup is clear and fruit shiny, about 2 hours. Bottle immediately in warm sterilised jars and seal, or cool and serve in glass dishes. Makes about 2 litres.

RIPE FIG JAM

3 kg ripe figs, peeled
500 ml water
1,5 kg sugar
100-120 ml lemon juice
10 ml ground ginger

Boil fruit in water until tender, about 10 minutes. Purée in a blender or food processor, then add sugar, lemon juice and ginger and heat slowly, stirring occasionally, until sugar has dissolved. Boil rapidly until thick, 10-15 minutes, skimming surface to remove scum. Pour into hot sterilised jars and seal immediately. Makes 3 kg.

QUINCE PRESERVE

Our favourite way to eat quinces when we were children was the following: Wash 1 quince very well and prick all over with a fork, making deep holes in it. Soak in lightly salted water for 6-12 hours before eating. Most of the time, we couldn't wait that long!

4 quinces
salted water
about 600 g sugar (depending on weight of
**   fruit)**
1 litre water
fresh ginger pieces

Peel quinces and remove seeds. Slice fruit. Wash in salted water, then soak in salted water to cover for about 6 hours, making sure that fruit is submerged, otherwise it will discolour. Boil sugar and water until a thick syrup forms, then add quince and ginger. Boil over medium heat until fruit is tender and syrup is thick, about 1½ hours. Pack fruit in hot sterilised jars, covering with syrup. Use immediately, or seal and store until needed. Makes about 600 g.

Note
• Weigh fruit to determine mass, and use same quantity of sugar.

The best Watermelon konfyt is made with a preserving watermelon like the one shown here. Dried sour figs (right) have to be well soaked before they are ready for using in Sour fig preserve.

Desserts and Beverages

BREAD PUDDING

A rich winter pudding and a good way of using up slightly stale bread.

4 slices white bread, crusts removed
600 ml milk
15 ml custard powder
50 ml sugar
4 eggs
5 ml vanilla essence
2 pieces stick cinnamon
3 cardamom seeds
50 ml butter

Quarter bread slices and soak in 200 ml milk. Mix a little milk with custard powder and 5 ml sugar to form a smooth paste. Heat remaining milk to boiling point. Add hot milk to custard paste, return to stove and stir to form a thin, runny custard. Beat eggs with remaining sugar and vanilla essence. Combine with custard and remaining ingredients, including the bread, and pour into a greased 23 cm diameter ovenproof dish. Bake at 180 °C for 30 minutes, or until set. Serve with hot Apricot sauce* or Gestoofde droë vrugte*. Serves 6.

APRICOT SAUCE

50 ml boiling water
60 ml smooth apricot jam

Combine water and jam to form a thin sauce. Use as a topping for Bread pudding* or Sago pudding* Makes about 100 ml.

Clockwise: **Sago pudding, Potato pudding, Gestoofde droë vrugte (page 70).**

SAGO PUDDING

A traditional pudding with a thick custardy texture. Many cooks have lost the art of making these nutritious puddings.

250 g sago
water for soaking
4 large eggs
3 pieces stick cinnamon
3 cardamom seeds, slightly bruised
150 g sugar
5 ml vanilla essence or rose water
600 ml milk
50 ml butter

Soak sago in water for 3 hours. Beat eggs well, then add cinnamon, cardamom seeds, sugar and vanilla essence or rose water. Add milk and mix well. Combine with sago and pour into a well-greased 2-litre ovenproof dish and dot with butter. Bake at 180 °C for 25 minutes, or until set. Serves 4-6.

Tapioca pudding: Use tapioca instead of sago, but soak for 6 hours.

TSCHIN-TSCHOU

Tschin-tschou or China grass jelly is made from strands of dried seaweed available from health stores and wholesale spice merchants.

50 g dried seaweed
250 ml water
5 ml vanilla essence or 15 ml rose water
pink food colouring
sugar to taste

Cook dried seaweed in 250 ml water until it has melted and the liquid is thick and syrupy, about 15 minutes. Add vanilla essence or rose water, food colouring and sugar. Stir well, pour into a glass bowl and refrigerate until set. Serves 4.

Variations
• Cook seaweed in 350 ml milk instead of water for a different texture.

• Crush jelly with a fork and add 50 ml to a milkshake made with 300 ml cold milk, 10 ml rose syrup and 5 ml falooda seeds.

POTATO PUDDING

This pudding is generally served at religious feasts and engagement parties. It is made in large trays cut into squares and is served with stewed fruit. The texture is firm and it cuts easily. Potato pudding makes a good substitute for melktert.

1 kg potatoes
50 ml butter
1 litre milk
10 eggs, well-beaten
125 ml sugar
5 ml salt
5 cardamom seeds
3 pieces stick cinnamon
10 ml vanilla essence
5 drops almond essence

Cook potatoes until soft, drain and mash with butter. Heat milk to lukewarm, then add to beaten eggs. Combine with mashed potatoes and stir in remaining ingredients. Pour into a well-greased ovenproof dish and bake at 180 °C for about 45 minutes, or until set and lightly golden. Serve with Gestoofde droë vrugte*. Serves 8-10.

Tameletjies served in modern cookie cups (left) and in traditional paper kadoesies *(right).*

GESTOOFDE PATATS

Stewed sweet potatoes with coconut brings back many childhood memories.

250 ml water
250 ml yellow sugar
50 ml butter
2 pieces stick cinnamon
3 ml ground dried naartjie peel
1 kg sweet potatoes, peeled and sliced

Bring water to boil in a heavy-based saucepan. Add yellow sugar, butter, cinnamon and naartjie peel and boil until thick and syrupy. Add sweet potatoes and cook over medium heat for about 15 minutes, or until tender. Serves 8.

Variation
• Stir in 100 ml desiccated coconut 5 minutes before serving.

GESKROEIDE VERMICELLI

Scorched vermicelli is an economical dish that goes far. It is a favourite pudding to serve during Ramadan.

250 g butter or margarine
3 pieces stick cinnamon
3 cardamom seeds, slightly bruised
100 ml sultanas
250 g vermicelli or lokshen
250 ml water
125 ml sugar, or to taste

Heat butter in a saucepan and add cinnamon, cardamom seeds, sultanas and vermicelli when foam subsides. Cook, tossing occasionally with a fork, until vermicelli turns golden brown, about 5 minutes. Add water and sugar and steam, covered, over medium heat until water has been absorbed, about 15 minutes, tossing now and then. Serves 8.

Variation
• Add 100 ml blanched almonds with the sultanas and spices.

TAMELETJIES

In the summer months when we were children we used to visit Vredehoek on the slopes of Table Mountain and search for pine kernels which fell from the stone pines.

500 ml water
1 kg sugar
2 pieces dried ginger
15 ml butter
500 ml pine kernels

Boil water, sugar and ginger until sticky and brown. Remove ginger. Stir in butter, then add pine kernels and stir to combine well. Pour mixture into individual rectangular paper cases (see below) or paper cookie cups to set. Makes about 500 g.

Note
•To make rectangular paper cases, called *kadoesies*, cut out paper rectangles 7 x 12 cm and fold up along each side to form a casing.

MELKTERT

Seventeenth century Malay cooks adapted the Dutch recipe for a basic custard pie by adding a feathering of ground nutmeg or cinnamon. Melktert is served at engagement parties and doopmaals.

600 g Biscuit pastry (page 77)

Filling
10 eggs
125 ml sugar
1 litre milk
30 ml custard powder
15 ml cake flour
5 ml sugar
10 ml vanilla essence
5 drops almond essence
2 pieces stick cinnamon
3 pods cardamom, slightly bruised
60 ml butter
3 ml ground cinnamon or nutmeg

Line a deep 40 x 30 cm oven dish with Biscuit pastry*. *Filling:* Beat eggs and 125 ml sugar until well-blended. Mix 50 ml milk to a paste with custard powder, flour and 5 ml sugar. Heat remaining milk to almost boiling, then stir into custard mixture. Return to stove and cook, stirring, to form a thin runny custard. Fold into egg mixture, add vanilla and almond essence, cinnamon sticks and carda-mom pods and mix well. Spoon filling into biscuit crust, dot with butter and sprinkle with cinnamon or nutmeg. Bake at 160 °C for 35-45 minutes, or until filling is set. Eat hot, cut into squares. Serves 16.

GRANNY'S FAVOURITE PUDDING

A delicious baked lemon pudding. Decorate with lemon leaves before baking for extra flavour.

100 ml butter
100 g castor sugar
2 large eggs, separated
250 ml self-raising flour
pinch salt
grated rind and juice of 1 large lemon
500 ml milk

Beat butter and sugar until light and creamy, then beat in yolks very well. Sift flour and salt together. Beat egg whites until stiff peaks form. Fold flour into yolk mixture with lemon rind and juice and 250 ml milk. Fold egg whites in lightly, then stir in remaining milk. Pour into a well-greased ovenproof dish and bake at 180 °C for 30-40 minutes, or until well-risen. The pudding makes a crusty top with a creamy lemon custard filling. Serves 4-6.

GESTOOFDE DROË VRUGTE

Stewed dried fruit is generally served as an accompaniment to baked puddings with the exception of melktert.

250 ml sugar
250 ml water
2 pieces stick cinnamon
250 g mixed dried fruit

Boil sugar, water and cinnamon until a thick syrup forms, about 15 minutes. Add dried fruit and cook on medium heat for a further 15 minutes. Serve with hot puddings. Serves 6.

CHILLED DESSERTS

Though not traditional, these desserts have become great favourites amongst our people, therefore no 'Malay' cookbook would be complete without them.

Granny's favourite pudding.

Left to right: *Granadilla milk jelly and Easy pineapple cheesecake.*

PINEAPPLE DESSERT

This is one of the first desserts I learned to make and it is still a favourite.

1 packet pineapple jelly
250 ml boiling water
1 x 410 g pineapple chunks, drained and reserve juice
1 x 410 g evaporated milk, chilled
125 ml fresh cream, whipped

Dissolve jelly in boiling water and reserved pineapple juice. Set aside to cool. Whip evaporated milk until thick and creamy, then add jelly and mix well. Stir in pineapple chunks reserving some for decoration. Pour into a large wetted mould and allow to set in refrigerator for at least 2 hours. Garnish with piped fresh cream and pineapple chunks. Serves 6-8.

EASY PINEAPPLE CHEESECAKE

1 packet pineapple jelly
250 ml boiling water
150 ml cold water
1 x 425 g can crushed pineapple
250 ml fresh cream
250 ml smooth cream cheese
1 packet Tennis biscuits
125 ml cream for garnishing
fresh pineapple for garnishing

Dissolve jelly in boiling water, then add cold water and mix well. Set aside to cool. Drain pineapple and reserve liquid. Beat fresh cream until thick, add cream cheese and blend well to combine. Add cold jelly and crushed pineapple and mix well. Dip tennis biscuits into pineapple juice then layer them into a square dish. Pour cream cheese mixture over biscuits. Crush remaining biscuits and sprinkle on top. Leave to set in refrigerator for about 1 hour. Beat remaining cream until stiff and pipe on top before serving. Garnish with slices of fresh pineapple if desired. Serves 6.

GRANADILLA MILK JELLY

1 packet granadilla jelly
250 ml condensed milk
100 ml granadilla pulp
125 ml fresh cream, whipped

Prepare jelly following instructions on packet and leave to cool. When jelly is cold, add condensed milk and granadilla pulp and beat well to combine. Pour into wetted jelly mould and allow to set. Turn out onto serving plate. Whip fresh cream until stiff peaks form. Decorate jelly with whipped cream. Serves 4-6.

Old fashioned trifle is an all-time favourite.

TRIFLE

1 x Swiss roll
1 packet raspberry jelly
1 packet greengage jelly
500 ml boiling water
300 ml cold water
1 x 425 g can fruit cocktail, drained
500 ml prepared custard
125 ml flaked almonds
250 fresh cream
10 glace cherries for garnishing
a few pieces of angelica for garnishing

In two separate containers dissolve each jelly in 250 ml hot water. Add 150 ml cold water and stir. Set aside to cool. Line bottom and sides of glass bowl with Swiss roll slices. Spoon 30 ml jelly over each slice, alternating the colours and allow jelly to soak in. Allow to set in freezer for about 20 minutes. Spoon well-drained fruit on top of Swiss roll slices, pour remaining green jelly over. Set in freezer, then pour red jelly on top and allow to set. Finally pour custard over and sprinkle with almonds, reserving some for decoration. Whip cream until stiff. Spread a layer of cream over the custard. Pipe remaining cream on top. Decorate with almonds, cherries and angelica. Leave in refrigerator to set for 2-3 hours. Serves 6-8.

STRAWBERRY YOGHURT JELLY

1 packet strawberry jelly
350 ml strawberry yoghurt
fresh strawberries for decoration

Prepare jelly following instructions on packet and allow to get thick and syrupy. Stir yoghurt into jelly and mix until well blended. Pour into wetted jelly mould. Allow to set until firm, about 1 hour, then turn out and garnish with fresh strawberries. Serves 6.

Variation

• Use different flavours of jelly and yoghurt.

CREAM PUFFS

Choux pastry
250 ml water
100 g butter or margarine
5 ml sugar
pinch of salt
250 ml sifted cake flour
4 eggs

Place water, butter, sugar and salt into a saucepan and bring to the boil. Add flour all at once, stirring vigorously until the mixture leaves the sides of the saucepan clean. Remove from heat and leave to cool until lukewarm. Beat in eggs one at a time and beat until smooth and well blended. Drop tablespoonsful of the mixture onto a greased baking sheet. Bake at 200 °C for 15 minutes, then reduce heat to 180 °C for a further 15 minutes. Switch off oven and allow puffs to dry until crisp. Remove from oven after 30 mintues and leave to cool on wire rack. Slit puffs in half and fill just before serving, otherise puffs will lose their crispness. Makes 24.

Chocolate filling

500 ml prepared chocolate instant pudding
125 ml fresh cream, whipped until stiff

Fill puffs with chocolate pudding followed by whipped cream. Dust with icing sugar.

Caramel banana filling

4 bananas, peeled and sliced
125 ml ready-made caramelised condensed milk
125 ml fresh cream, whipped until stiff

Fill each puff with 2 slices banana, 5 ml caramelised condensed milk and 10 ml whipped cream. Dust with icing sugar.

Fruit cocktail filling

1 x 425 g can fruit cocktail, well drained
125 ml fresh cream, whipped

Fill puffs with 10 ml diced canned fruit and 10 ml whipped cream. Dust with icing sugar.

Beverages

FALOODA MILKSHAKE

A delicious rose-flavoured milkshake. Rose syrup, a dark pink, very sweet syrup, is available from spice shops.

500 ml milk
5 ml rose syrup
2 scoops vanilla ice-cream (optional)
15 ml grated falooda jelly*
5 ml falooda seeds, soaked in 30 ml water for 15 minutes and drained
pink food colouring (optional)

Combine milk, rose syrup and ice-cream in a blender. Add falooda jelly and seeds and a few drops food colouring. Blend until well-combined and serve cold. Serves 4.

Note
• To make falooda jelly, boil 30 ml tschin-tschou (dried seaweed jelly) in 250 ml water until thick and syrupy, about 15 minutes. Add pink food colouring to taste, if desired, strain through a fine-mesh sieve and set in the refrigerator. Grate jelly finely and use as required.

BOEBER

A thick, spicy milk drink always served hot on the 15th night of Ramadan to celebrate the middle of the fast. For a thicker boeber, add more sago.

125 g butter
250 ml vermicelli
10 cardamom seeds, bruised
3 pieces stick cinnamon
50 g sultanas
2 litres milk
75 ml sago, soaked in 200 ml water for 30 minutes
100 ml sweetened condensed milk
15 ml rosewater or 10 ml vanilla essence
150 ml sugar, or to taste
50 g blanched almonds (optional)

Melt butter in a deep saucepan, add vermicelli and toss with a fork until lightly browned. Add cardamom, cinnamon and sultanas, then pour in milk and bring to boil. Stir in presoaked sago and simmer until sago is transparent, about 15 minutes, stirring occasionally to prevent sticking. Mix in condensed milk, rosewater or vanilla essence, sugar and almonds and simmer until well-blended, about 10 minutes. Serve hot. Serves 8-10.

CARDAMOM TEA

Milky tea with a spicy flavour. A pinch of ground ginger may also be added.

1 litre water
500 ml milk
4-5 tea bags
3 cardamom seeds, bruised
sugar to taste

Bring water and milk to boil in a stainless steel teapot. Add tea bags and cardamom seeds and simmer for 1 minute to allow tea and spices to draw. Remove tea bags and pour into teacups, through a strainer. Serve with sugar to taste. Serves 4-6.

LEMONADE

A refreshing summer drink making use of lemons which are freely available at this time of year.

4 large ripe lemons
300 g sugar
125 ml water

Wash lemons well and grate rind of 1. Squeeze juice from lemons and strain through a fine-mesh sieve. Combine sugar and water in a saucepan, stir in lemon rind and heat over low heat until sugar dissolves. Bring to boil, then simmer for 5 minutes. Cool and add strained lemon juice. Store in the refrigerator. Dilute lemon syrup with soda water or iced water (1 part lemon syrup to 2 parts water) and serve on crushed ice with a sprig of mint. Serves 4.

PAWPAW AND APPLE JUICE

An unusual fruit drink, with a tropical flavour.

1 ripe medium pawpaw, peeled, seeded and sliced
3 Granny Smith apples, peeled, cored and sliced
200 ml unsweetened guava juice

Liquidise pawpaw and apples in a blender or food processor and stir in guava juice. Serve with ice cubes. Pawpaw and apple juice will keep for up to 1 week in the refrigerator. Makes about 1 litre.

SPARKLING FRUIT PUNCH

Just right for a party.

1 ripe pineapple
2 oranges
1 large lemon
100 ml granadilla pulp
500 ml granadilla squash
1,5 litres sparkling orange cool drink
1 litre soda water
mint leaves for decoration

Peel and purée pineapple. Wash oranges and lemon well and slice very thinly. Combine pineapple purée, granadilla pulp, granadilla squash, orange cool drink and soda water in a large punch bowl. Stir to blend. Add orange and lemon slices and mint leaves and add ice cubes just before serving. Makes about 4 litres.

FLOU TEE

Weak black tea with a slice of lemon, usually served after fish dishes or very fatty or spicy foods. Slices of orange may be used instead of lemon.

1 tea bag
1 litre boiling water
1 small lemon, sliced
sugar to taste

Place tea bag in a teapot and pour boiling water over. Allow to draw for about 1 minute, then discard tea bag and pour tea into cups. Serve with sliced lemon and sugar to taste. Serves 4.

A typical Thursday night prayer meeting where Boeber (centre), Gedatmelk (foreground) and Geskroeide vermicelli (right) could be served along with Samoosas and Twisted doughnuts (left).

GEDATMELK

Gedatmelk is generally served after the gedat (ghajad), special prayers usually held on Thursday or Sunday nights. It resembles boeber in taste but is not as thick or as rich.

5 ml ground cinnamon
10 cardamom seeds, bruised
2 litres milk
sugar to taste
a few drops rosewater (optional)

Tie cinnamon and cardamom seeds in a muslin bag. Immerse in 1 litre milk in a saucepan and bring to boil. Remove from stove and allow spices to draw for 15 minutes. Remove muslin bag and add remaining milk, sugar and rosewater if using. Serve in small glasses. Makes 2 litres.

Biscuits

MYMOENA'S ALMOND BISCUITS

Buttery biscuits with a crisp texture.

200 ml sugar
250 g butter
250 ml very finely chopped almonds
30 ml cornflour
500 ml cake flour, sifted
5 drops almond essence

Cream sugar and butter until soft and well-blended. Add remaining ingredients and mix to a soft dough. Roll dough out to 3 mm thick on a lightly floured surface and scrape top with a fork to give a rough texture. Cut out rounds and place on lightly greased baking sheets. Bake at 200 °C for about 10 minutes, or until lightly browned. Makes about 60.

BISCUIT PASTRY

This pastry is ideal for fruit tarts and a melk-tert base.

200 ml castor sugar
30 ml sunflower oil
250 g butter or margarine
2 eggs
5 ml vanilla or lemon essence
500 ml cake flour, sifted
500 ml self-raising flour

Cream sugar, oil and butter together until well-blended. Add eggs and essence and stir to blend. Fold in flours and mix to a soft dough. Use as a crust for pies and tarts. Makes about 600 g.

From left to right: *Mary Annes, Mymoena's almond biscuits, Lemoenkoek, and Butter biscuits decorated with cherries and angelica.*

ANGEL WHISPERS

These are light, crumbly biscuits very much like Melting moments.

125 g butter
125 g castor sugar
5 ml vanilla essence
2 eggs, lightly beaten
30 ml evaporated milk
500 ml cake flour
60 ml cornflour
pinch salt
strawberry or raspberry jam
icing sugar

Cream butter until soft. Add sugar and cream until light and fluffy and no longer grainy. Add vanilla essence and beat well. Beat in eggs, then add evaporated milk. Sift cake flour, cornflour and salt together and stir into creamed mixture to make a fairly stiff dough. Break off small pieces of dough and roll into balls. Place balls on greased baking sheets and flatten with a fork. Bake at 200 °C for 8-10 minutes or until lightly browned. Allow to cool slightly, then sandwich 2 biscuits together with strawberry or raspberry jam and sprinkle with icing sugar. Makes about 30 pairs.

BUTTER BISCUITS

Traditional Malay biscuits.

250 g butter
100 ml sunflower oil
250 ml castor sugar
10 ml vanilla essence
1 large egg, beaten
500 g cake flour
10 ml baking powder
angelica and glacé cherries for decoration

Cream butter until soft, then stir in oil. Add sugar and beat until light and fluffy and no longer grainy. Add vanilla essence and beat well. Beat in egg. Sift cake flour and baking powder and stir into creamed mixture to make a fairly stiff dough. Roll out dough to 3 mm thick on a lightly floured surface and cut out shapes with biscuit cutters. Place on lightly greased baking sheets. Decorate biscuits with angelica and glacé cherries and bake at 200 °C for 8-10 minutes or until lightly browned. Makes 80.

Mary Annes: Use 15 ml ground aniseed and strawberry or pineapple essence instead of vanilla essence. Decorate with hundreds and thousands.
Lemoenkoek: Use orange essence instead of vanilla, add 5 ml finely grated orange rind and decorate with strips of orange peel.

FAWZIA'S SOETKOEKIES

The oil is the only modern ingredient in this traditional recipe. In the past, sheeptail fat would have been used. Red boll is a ferri-oxide mixture obtainable from chemists.

250 g butter
100 ml sunflower oil
500 ml yellow or brown sugar
5 ml ground cloves
5 ml ground ginger
2 ml ground mixed spice
1 egg, lightly beaten
250 ml ground almonds (optional)
500 g cake flour
5 ml bicarbonate of soda
red boll for colouring
peanut halves for decoration

Cream butter until soft. Stir in oil until well-blended. Add sugar and cream until light and fluffy. Stir in cloves, ginger and mixed spice, then beat in egg. Stir in ground almonds, if using. Sift flour and bicarbonate of soda and stir into mixture to make a fairly stiff dough. Mix red boll with a third of the dough, until well-blended. Roll out remaining two-thirds on a lightly floured surface, dot with pieces of red-coloured dough and roll out to 4 mm thick. Cut into fancy shapes with a biscuit cutter and place on greased baking sheets. Decorate with peanut halves and bake at 200 °C for 10-12 minutes or until golden. Makes 80-100.

Post toasties biscuits are a favourite with children.

ROMANY CREAMS

250 ml sugar
200 g butter or margarine
65 ml sunflower oil
2 eggs
65 ml cocoa powder
500 g cake flour
5 ml baking powder
pinch salt
250 g desiccated coconut
200 g baking chocolate

Cream sugar, butter or margarine and oil. Add eggs and mix to combine well. Sift cocoa powder, cake flour, baking powder and salt and add, with coconut, to creamed mixture. Mix to a fairly stiff dough. Roll out on a lightly floured surface to about 5 mm thick. Scrape top of dough with a fork for a rough texture. Cut out rounds, about 5 cm in diameter, and place on greased baking sheets. Bake at 180 °C for 12-15 minutes. Cool on a wire rack. Melt chocolate over a basin of hot water and sandwich pairs of biscuits with chocolate. Makes about 50.

Variation
• Do not sandwich biscuits. Drop about 5 ml melted chocolate on top of each and decorate with a chocolate Smartie.

LATIEFA'S COCONUT MACAROONS

1 egg white
150 ml castor sugar
250 ml desiccated coconut
pinch salt
5 ml cold water (optional)
glacé cherries for decoration

Whisk egg white until quite stiff, then beat in sugar, coconut and salt gradually. Add cold water if mixture is too stiff. Line baking sheets with greased waxproof paper and drop spoonfuls of mixture, about 10 ml at a time, on paper. Bake at 200 °C for about 10 minutes, or until very lightly browned. Decorate with halved glacé cherries. Makes about 36.

POST TOASTIES BISCUITS

500 g butter
150 ml sunflower oil
500 g castor sugar
3 large eggs
10 ml ground cardamom
15 ml ground ginger
500 ml chopped dates
100 g walnuts, chopped
1 kg cake flour
500 ml crushed Post Toasties

Cream butter until soft. Stir in oil until well-blended. Add castor sugar and cream until light and fluffy. Beat in eggs, then stir in cardamom, ginger, dates and walnuts. Sift cake flour and stir into mixture to make a fairly stiff dough. Roll out to 3 mm thick on a lightly floured surface and scrape surface with a fork for a rough texture. Cut out star shapes with a biscuit cutter and coat tops with crushed Post Toasties, pressing in firmly with your fingers. Place on greased baking sheets and bake at 200 °C for 10-12 minutes, or until golden. Makes about 150.

Soraya's choc crusts.

SORAYA'S CHOC CRUSTS

These ginger and coconut biscuits are some of my favourites.

250 g butter or margarine
150 ml sunflower oil
400 ml castor sugar
10 ml smooth apricot jam
25 ml golden syrup
15 ml ground ginger
1 egg, lightly beaten
750 ml desiccated coconut
600 g cake flour
10 ml bicarbonate of soda
300 g baking chocolate, melted

Cream butter or margarine until soft. Stir in oil to blend, then beat in castor sugar until light and fluffy. Stir in apricot jam, golden syrup and ginger, then beat in egg until well-blended. Stir in coconut. Sift flour and bicarbonate of soda and stir into mixture to form a fairly stiff dough. Roll out to 3 mm thick on a lightly floured surface and scrape with a fork to give a rough texture. Cut out with a round 5 cm diameter biscuit cutter. Place on greased baking sheets and bake at 200 °C for 8-10 minutes, or until lightly browned. Allow to cool slightly, then spread with melted chocolate. Makes 80.

ZUBEIDA'S COCONUT CRISPS

200 g butter
250 ml castor sugar
10 ml lemon juice
1 egg, beaten
500 ml self-raising flour
250 ml desiccated coconut
extra desiccated coconut for rolling
glacé cherries, quartered, for decoration

Cream butter, castor sugar and lemon juice. Add beaten egg and mix well. Add flour and coconut and mix until mixture is soft and a little sticky. Break off small pieces of dough and roll them into walnut-sized balls. Roll balls in extra coconut and place on well-greased baking sheets. Flatten them slightly with a fork. Place cherry quarters on each biscuit and bake at 200 °C for 15 minutes or until lightly browned. Makes about 40.

ZAIDA'S CHOC MINT CRISPS

Crispy chocolate coconut biscuits which are very easy to make.

250 g butter
60 ml sunflower oil
250 ml sugar
50 ml cocoa powder
400 ml desiccated coconut
500 ml cake flour
5 ml baking powder
2 x 50 g peppermint crisp chocolate bars, grated

Cream butter until soft. Stir in oil until well-blended. Add sugar and cream until light and fluffy. Stir in cocoa powder and coconut. Sift flour and baking powder and stir into mixture to make a fairly soft dough. Press into a greased baking sheet and bake at 200 °C for 8-10 minutes or until golden. Cut into squares while still warm and sprinkle with grated peppermint crisp. Cool before removing from baking sheet.
Makes 36-40

KRAPKOEKIES

Spicy biscuits with the subtle flavour of naartjie peel.

200 g butter
65 ml sunflower oil
250 ml sugar
1 egg
500 g cake flour
pinch salt
8 ml ground cardamom
5 ml ground cinnamon
5 ml ground dried naartjie peel
250 g desiccated coconut
100 g glacé orange peel cut into squares
**   for decoration**

Cream butter, oil and sugar. Mix in egg. Sift flour, salt, cardamom, cinnamon and naartjie peel and add to creamed mixture. Add coconut and mix to a fairly stiff dough. Roll out to 6 mm thick on a lightly floured surface and scrape top with a fork for a rough texture. Cut out shapes with biscuit cutters and place on greased baking sheets. Decorate with pieces of glacé orange peel and bake at 180 °C for 12-15 minutes or until golden brown. Cool on wire racks. Makes 96.

KARAMONK SCRAPS

Cardamom biscuits are another Malay favourite.

200 g butter
65 ml sunflower oil
250 ml sugar
2 eggs
500 g cake flour
5 ml baking powder
15 ml ground cardamom
5 ml ground dried ginger
5 ml ground cinnamon
50 g peanuts or mixed peel for decoration

Cream butter, oil and sugar. Beat in eggs. Sift flour, baking powder and spices. Add to creamed mixture and knead to a fairly stiff dough. Roll out to 6 mm thick on a lightly floured surface and scrape top with a fork for a rough texture. Cut into rectangles or crescent shapes and place on greased baking sheets. Decorate with halved peanuts or mixed peel and bake at 180 °C for 12-15 minutes or until golden brown. Cool on wire racks. Makes 72.

SABOERA

Very traditional biscuits flavoured with rosewater and distinctively decorated with three currants.

200 g butter
65 ml sunflower oil
250 ml sugar
500 g cake flour
5 ml baking powder
pinch salt
5 ml rosewater
125 ml sugar
50 g currants for decoration

Cream butter, oil and sugar. Sift flour, baking powder and salt and combine with creamed mixture. Mix in rosewater and knead to a farily stiff dough. Roll out to 5 mm thick on a lightly floured surface and cut into rectangular shapes about 3 cm x 6 cm. Dip each in sugar and place on greased baking sheets. Arrange 3 currants on each, in lengthwise rows. Bake at 180 °C for 12-15 minutes or until golden brown. Cool on wire racks. Makes 72.

JAM RINGS

A modern recipe which has found its place in the Malay community. If you don't have vanilla sugar, add 5 ml vanilla essence and 25 g castor sugar.

400 g cake flour
200 g cold butter, flaked
3 egg yolks
100 g castor sugar
25 g vanilla-flavoured sugar
50 g ground almonds
finely grated rind and juice of 1 lemon
100 g strawberry jam
icing sugar

Sift flour into a mixing bowl and add butter. Place egg yolks, sugar, vanilla sugar, almonds and lemon rind in centre and knead all ingredients to a dough. Wrap in waxproof paper and chill in the refrigerator for 2 hours. Roll dough out to 5 mm thick on a lightly floured surface and cut out equal numbers of circles and rings about 5 cm in diameter with pastry cutters. Place circles and rings on greased baking sheets and bake at 200 °C for about 10 minutes, or until golden. Lift carefully off baking sheets and cool on a wire rack. Combine strawberry jam with lemon juice and spread onto round biscuits. Sift icing sugar onto ring biscuits

and carefully place a ring biscuit on each of the jam-covered round biscuits. Makes 50.

Cook's tip
• To make vanilla sugar, store 2 vanilla pods with 500 g sugar in a sealed container for at least 1 week. The longer you store the vanilla pods in the sugar, the stronger the flavour.

COCONUT SCRAPS

'Scraps' is another name for crisply baked biscuits.

500 g butter
200 ml sugar
1 egg
2 ml ground nutmeg or 7 drops almond
**   essence**
750 g flour
2 ml baking powder
pinch salt
650 ml desiccated coconut
125 ml sugar
50 g quartered glacé cherries or silver balls
**   for decoration**

Cream butter and sugar well. Mix in egg, then add nutmeg or almond essence. Sift flour, baking powder and salt and add to creamed mixture with coconut. Knead to a fairly stiff dough and roll out to 6 mm thick on a lightly floured surface. Scrape top with a fork for a rough texture. Cut out star shapes and dip in sugar. Place on greased baking sheets, decorate with cherries or silver balls and bake at 180 °C for 12-15 minutes, or until golden brown. Cool on wire racks. Makes about 120.

These favourite biscuits – Saboeras, Coconut scraps and Krapkoekies – are sometimes used for a barakat, seen here in the background. This gift, beautifully wrapped, is similar to the ones presented to the bridegroom's relatives at engagements.

Koesisters, Fritters and Breads

DOUGHNUTS

These light textured doughnuts are a firm family favourite, taking the place of the more traditional koesisters.

65 ml sugar
60 ml melted butter or margarine
125 ml boiling water
15 ml active dried yeast
1 egg, beaten
125 ml milk
500 g cake flour
15 ml baking powder
pinch bicarbonate of soda
pinch salt
5 ml vanilla essence
750 ml sunflower oil
sugar syrup*

Combine sugar, butter and boiling water and, when cooled, add yeast. Stir in beaten egg and milk. Sift flour and baking powder, then add, with bicarbonate of soda, salt and vanilla essence, to butter mixture. Mix to a very soft dough. Set aside to rise, covered, until doubled in bulk, about 2 hours. Roll dough out into a thick coil about 5 cm in diameter and cut off 3 cm strips. Shape into longish doughnuts or ring doughnuts and set aside for 30 minutes to rise again. Fry in moderately hot oil for about 5 minutes on each side, or until lightly browned. Drain in a colander or on absorbent paper. Dip doughnuts, 1-2 at a time, into hot syrup and cook for 1 minute. Remove with a slotted spoon and drain. Makes 50.

Cream doughnuts: Do not dip doughnuts in sugar syrup but coat in glacé icing, made by combining 250 ml icing sugar and 60 ml water. Halve doughnuts (but do not cut right through) and spread strawberry or mixed fruit jam on insides, then pipe 250 ml whipped fresh cream over jam.

From top to bottom: *Rille gebak, currant bollas and jam-filled bollas.*

BOLLAS

Bollas are like small, round doughnuts dipped in a sugary syrup. Traditionally they were served plain, but nowadays they can be rolled in coconut or filled with jam.

25 ml butter or margarine
20 ml sugar
2 eggs
500 ml cake flour
500 ml self-raising flour
5 ml baking powder
pinch salt
5 ml vanilla essence
400 ml milk
500 ml sunflower oil
sugar syrup*

Melt butter, add to sugar and eggs in a bowl and beat well. Sift flours, baking powder and salt and add to butter mixture. Add vanilla essence and milk and mix to a thick batter. Heat oil to moderately hot in a medium deep saucepan. Dip a tablespoon in hot water and scoop up some batter. Drop spoonfuls into hot oil and deep-fry until lightly browned, 5-8 minutes. Remove with a slotted spoon and drain in a colander. Dip drained bollas in hot sugar syrup and drain. Serve hot or cold. Makes 40.

Variations
• Add 100 ml washed currants to batter before frying.
• After dipping bollas in sugar syrup, roll them in desiccated coconut.
• Instead of dipping in sugar syrup, make an incision in each bolla and spoon in 5 ml apricot jam, then roll it in castor sugar.

SUGAR SYRUP

500 ml water
250 ml sugar
pinch bicarbonate of soda
10 ml butter

Bring water and sugar to boil and boil until sugar has dissolved and syrup is slightly thickened. Stir in bicarbonate of soda and butter and use as a dipping syrup for Koesisters*, Bollas* and other recipes. Makes 750 ml.

RILLE GEBAK

These rich sweetmeats, like heavy doughnuts, are distinctively diamond shaped. This is an old recipe passed on to me by my grandmother, who for years kept it a well guarded secret. In the past, sheeptail fat would have been used instead of oil.

250 ml yellow or brown sugar
200 g butter
60 ml sunflower oil
2 large eggs, beaten well
500 g self-raising flour
250 ml cake flour
2 ml salt
5 ml baking powder
10 ml ground dried ginger
10 ml ground cardamom
10 ml ground cinnamon
10 ml ground naartjie peel
350 ml milk
2 ml bicarbonate of soda
750 ml sunflower oil

Cinnamon sugar
250 ml sugar
10 ml ground cinnamon

Cream sugar, butter and oil very well. Mix in beaten egg. Sift flours, salt and baking powder into a mixing bowl and add spices. Stir into butter mixture alternately with milk mixed with bicarbonate of soda, adding more milk if mixture seems too stiff. Knead to a soft dough, then roll out onto a lightly floured surface to 5 mm thick. Cut out diamond shapes and fry in deep hot oil for about 5 minutes on either side, or until lightly browned. Drain on absorbent paper or in a colander and dip in sugar mixed with ground cinnamon. Makes 40.

KOESISTERS

Sunday mornings wouldn't be the same without koesisters for breakfast. I remember, as a child in District Six, spending Saturdays preparing koesisters for the next morning. Often, too, you would see children hawking koesisters in the streets, going from house to house with their baskets. Malay koesisters are not plaited, but are oblong in shape, light and puffy and very spicy.

500 g cake flour
100 ml self-raising flour
100 ml sugar
2 ml salt
10 ml ground ginger
5 ml ground cinnamon
10 ml ground aniseed
5 ml ground cardamom
10 ml ground dried naartjie peel (optional)
125 ml sunflower oil
1 egg
250 ml cold milk
250 ml hot water
20 ml active dried yeast
5 ml sugar
750 ml sunflower oil
sugar syrup*
150 ml desiccated coconut

Sift flours, sugar and salt into a mixing bowl and stir in spices and naartjie peel. Rub in 125 ml oil to form a crumbly mixture. Mix milk and water and dissolve yeast and sugar in half the milk mixture. Add to flour with egg and remaining milk mixture. Mix to a soft dough. Moisten hands with oil and rub over dough, then set dough aside, covered, to rise until doubled in bulk, about 2 hours. Roll dough out to a 5 cm thick coil on an oiled surface. Cut off 2 cm lengths and shape each into a slightly flattened doughnut shape. Set aside, covered, for 30 minutes to rise again. Heat oil in a saucepan and fry koesisters for 5 minutes on each side, or until browned. Drain on absorbent paper or in a colander. Boil koesisters, a few at a time, in sugar syrup for 1 minute, then drain and sprinkle with coconut. Makes 60.

Variation
• Make a firm coconut topping by boiling 250 ml coconut, 125 ml sugar, 1 piece stick cinnamon, 2 cardamom seeds and 50 ml water in a small saucepan until coconut is shiny and well-blended with sugar, stirring occasionally. Remove cinnamon and cardamom seeds and place about 5 ml mixture in centre of each koesister after it has been boiled in sugar syrup.

TWISTED POTATO DOUGHNUTS

The potato in this recipe makes the dough nice and light.

15 ml active dried yeast
65 ml lukewarm water
5 ml sugar
2 medium potatoes
10 ml butter
120 ml sugar
45 ml melted butter
1 egg, beaten
750 ml cake flour
pinch salt
10 ml ground dried naartjie peel
750 ml sunflower oil
sugar syrup*
100 ml desiccated coconut

Dissolve yeast in water with 5 ml sugar. Peel and boil potatoes until tender, then mash with butter. Beat remaining sugar, melted butter and egg until well-combined and add mashed potatoes. Mix well. Stir in yeast mixture. Sift flour and salt and add to potato mixture with naartjie peel. Mix to a soft dough. Set aside, covered, until doubled in bulk, about 2 hours. Roll dough out on an oiled surface to a coil 5 cm in diameter, cut off 3 cm lengths and roll each into a thinner coil. Twist each coil and leave to rise, covered, for 30 minutes. Heat oil in a saucepan and fry doughnuts for 5 minutes on each side, or until lightly browned. Boil doughnuts in syrup for 1 minute then drain on absorbent paper or in a colander. Sprinkle with desiccated coconut. Makes 40.

COPENHAGENS

A modern favourite made with a yeast dough.

600 g cake flour
125 ml sugar
125 g softened butter
20 ml active dried yeast
250 ml lukewarm milk
5 ml sugar
2 eggs, beaten
250 ml sultanas or fruit cake mixture
150 ml yellow sugar
1 egg, lightly beaten
250 ml icing sugar
30 ml water

Sift flour into a mixing bowl and stir in sugar. Rub in softened butter until mixture is crumbly. Dissolve yeast in milk with 5 ml sugar. Make a well in flour, stir in eggs and yeast mixture and mix to a soft dough. Set aside, covered, to rise until doubled in bulk, about 2 hours. Roll dough out into a long coil on a lightly floured surface. Cut off 4 cm lengths and roll each out into a circle about 12 cm in diameter. Sprinkle each with 5 ml sultanas and 2 ml yellow sugar and roll into a long thin coil. Roll dough up into a circle, from one side only, and tuck end underneath. Set aside, covered, for 30 minutes to rise again. Brush with beaten egg and bake at 200 °C for about 15 minutes, or until lightly browned. Mix icing sugar and water to a paste and drip about 5 ml onto each copenhagen while it's still hot. Makes 36.

PANCAKES

Delicious rolled-up pancakes with a coconut filling. Alternatively fill with jam and cream or with cinnamon sugar.

500 ml self-raising flour
2 ml grated nutmeg
2 ml salt
2 eggs, beaten well
50 ml melted butter
500 ml milk
30 ml sunflower oil

Filling
250 ml desiccated coconut
125 ml sugar
1 piece stick cinnamon
2 cardamom seeds
50 ml water

Sift flour into a mixing bowl, then stir in nutmeg and salt. Beat eggs, butter and milk and gradually add flour mixture, beating constantly, to form a smooth thin batter. Set aside for at least 1 hour. Heat a heavy-based frying pan and grease lightly with oil. Pour a thin layer of batter into pan, tilting it to distribute batter evenly. Fry on one side until browned, 1-2 minutes, then turn over with a spatula and brown on other side. Turn out into a casserole dish and keep warm, covered, in the oven while making other pancakes. *Filling:* Boil all ingredients in a small saucepan until coconut is shiny and well-blended with sugar. Remove cinnamon and cardamom seeds. Place about 10 ml filling on each pancake, roll up and serve hot. Makes 30.

Koesisters made the traditional way.

VETBROODJIES

These make an ideal substitute for bread especially when we go camping during the summer.

500 ml cake flour
10 ml baking powder
5 ml salt
2 eggs, beaten well
250 ml milk
15 ml melted butter
500 ml sunflower oil

Sift flour, baking powder and salt into a mixing bowl. Combine eggs, milk and melted butter separately and add to flour mixture. Stir well to make a smooth thick batter. heat oil in a deep frying pan or saucepan and drop batter, 15 ml at a time, into it. Fry for 2 minutes on one side, or until golden, then turn with a slotted spoon and fry other side until brown, about 1 minute. Drain in a colander and serve with jam or leftover Mince curry*. Makes about 20.

BANANA VETKOEKIES

Banana fritters were once fried in sheeptail fat but are now fried in sunflower oil and drained well. The deeper the oil the more the fritters will puff.

500 ml self-raising flour
pinch salt
15 ml sugar
1 egg, lightly beaten
30 ml melted butter or margarine
5 ml banana essence
200 ml milk
4 large ripe bananas
400 ml sunflower oil
cinnamon sugar*

Sift flour and salt into a bowl and stir in 15 ml sugar. Make a well in centre and add egg, butter, banana essence and milk. Mix to a thick pancake batter. Peel and coarsely chop bananas and add to mixture. Stir to combine well. Heat oil in a large frying pan and drop batter, 15 ml at a time, into it. Fry fritters until golden brown, about 3 minutes on either side. Drain on absorbent paper and sprinkle with cinnamon sugar*. Serve hot. Makes 36.

Pumpkin fritters: Omit bananas and banana essence and add 250 ml mashed cooked pumpkin.

WHOLEWHEAT LOAF

A modern recipe for a health-giving loaf. Once you have mastered this recipe you will be able to vary it by adding sultanas or sunflower seeds to it.

500 g wholewheat flour
5 ml salt
10 ml instant dried yeast
30 ml sunflower oil
20 ml honey or golden syrup
325 ml lukewarm water

Place flour and salt in a bowl. Add instant dried yeast and stir. Add oil and honey or golden syrup, then water. Mix to a soft dough and knead until elastic. Form into a smooth loaf shape and place in a well-greased loaf tin. Cover with plastic and leave to rise until doubled in bulk, 45 minutes-1 hour. Bake at 220 °C for 30 minutes, then reduce temperature to 200 °C and bake a further 10-15 minutes. To test if loaf is baked, tap it on top – it should sound hollow. Cool in tin for a few minutes, then turn out onto a wire rack to cool completely. Makes 1 large loaf.

Note
• Active dried yeast may also be used. Dissolve yeast in 150 ml of the lukewarm water with 2 ml sugar and leave until bubbling, about 15 minutes. Add to dry ingredients, with remaining water, and proceed as above.

MILK ROLLS

Feathery light rolls ideal for a picnic or braai.

700 g cake flour
100 g self-raising flour
5 ml salt
20 ml sugar
100 g butter or margarine
1 x 10 g packet instant dried yeast
250 ml lukewarm milk
150 ml lukewarm water
1 egg, lightly beaten
15 ml milk

Mix flours, salt and sugar with butter or margarine to make a crumbly mixture. Add instant dried yeast and stir. Combine milk and water, add to flour mixture and knead

very well. Add more water if necessary – dough should be fairly soft. Moisten hands with oil and smooth over dough. Cover dough with plastic and leave to rise in a warm place until doubled in bulk, about 1½-2 hours. Punch down and shape into desired shapes. Pack onto greased baking sheets, leaving enough space between them for rolls to rise. Set aside, covered, for about 30 minutes to rise again. Combine beaten egg and milk and use to coat tops of rolls. Bake at 180 °C for 20-25 minutes, or until risen and lightly golden on top. Leave to cool on sheets for about 5 minutes, then turn out onto wire racks to cool completely. Makes about 24.

Note
• Active dried yeast may also be used. Mix with 5 ml sugar and the 150 ml lukewarm water and leave until bubbling about 15 minutes. Add to dry ingredients, then add milk and proceed as above.

ANISEED RAISIN LOAF

An easy-to-make loaf which doesn't use yeast.

250 ml cake flour
750 ml self-raising flour
pinch salt
10 ml baking powder
20 ml coarsely ground aniseeds
250 ml seedless raisins
2 eggs
125 ml sugar
30 ml sunflower oil
500 ml milk

Glaze
50 ml sugar
50 ml hot water

Grease and line a large loaf tin. Sift flours, salt and baking powder into a large bowl. Stir in aniseed and raisins. Beat eggs and sugar separately in a large mixing bowl until light and fluffy, then add oil and beat well. Add flour mixture alternately with milk, mixing after each addition to combine well. Pour mixture into lined loaf tin and bake at 180 °C for 45-55 minutes. Leave in tin for 10 minutes, then turn out onto a wire rack. *Glaze:* Dissolve sugar in water and brush over top of raisin loaf. Leave to cool. Serve buttered. Makes 1 large loaf.

Clockwise: ***Banana vetkoekies,***
Wholewheat loaf and Aniseed raisin loaf.

Cakes and Pastries

GLACÉ FRUIT TRIEM

This rich fruit cake is expensive to make and considered a luxury. It is generally served for special occasions like Eid Labarang, the first day after Ramadan.

50 g glacé cherries
250 g fruit cake mix
250 g mixed whole glacé fruit (pineapple, figs, watermelon)
750 ml self-raising flour
10 ml baking powder
5 ml salt
5 ml ground cinnamon
100 g walnuts, chopped
250 ml brown sugar
200 g butter
4 large eggs
60 ml sunflower oil
60 ml golden syrup
10 ml vanilla essence
125 ml cream

Halve cherries and pick over fruit cake mix. Chop mixed glacé fruit. Sift flour, baking powder, salt and cinnamon into a bowl and stir in nuts, cherries and fruit to coat well with flour. Cream sugar and butter until light and fluffy. Add eggs, one at a time, beating well after each addition. Add oil and mix well. Stir in golden syrup and vanilla essence, then add flour mixture and cream and mix very well. Grease and line a large deep square cake tin and pour mixture into it. Bake at 180 °C for 45 minutes, then reduce temperature to i60 °C and bake for a further 45 mintues. Test with a thin skewer; if it comes out clean the cake is done. Leave in switched-off oven for 15 minutes before turning out onto a wire rack to cool. Makes 1 large cake.

Clockwise: *Cherry triem, Glacé fruit triem, and Cinnamon and carrot cake.*

SPICY DATE AND WALNUT TRIEM

A rich, dark date loaf.

750 ml cake flour
5 ml baking powder
5 ml ground cinnamon
150 ml boiling water
150 g stoned dates, chopped
5 ml bicarbonate of soda
225 g butter or margarine
250 ml sugar
3 eggs, beaten
100 g walnuts, chopped

Grease and line a large loaf tin. Sift flour, baking powder and cinnamon into a bowl. Pour boiling water into a bowl, add dates and sprinkle with bicarbonate of soda. Set aside for 15 minutes, or until cool. Cream butter or margarine and sugar until light and fluffy, then add beaten eggs and mix well. Add flour mixture, dates and walnuts and mix to a soft dropping consistency. Pour into loaf tin and bake at 170 °C for 1¼-1½ hours, on middle shelf of oven. Allow to stand in tin for 10 minutes, then turn out onto a wire rack to cool. Makes 1 large loaf.

CHERRY TRIEM

This is an old recipe given to me by my grandmother.

100 g cake flour
100 g self-raising flour
pinch salt
175 g butter
175 g castor sugar
4 large eggs
5 drops almond essence
15 ml milk
100 g cherries, halved and tossed in 30 ml cake flour
icing sugar or castor sugar for decoration

Grease and line an 18 cm diameter cake tin. Sift flours and salt into a bowl. Cream butter and sugar until light and fluffy. Whisk eggs lightly and add gradually to creamed mixture, beating well after each addition. Scrape down sides of bowl and beat again. Stir in almond essence, then gradually add sifted flour, folding in after each addition. Stir in milk to give a soft dropping consistency, then stir in cherries, distributing them well. Pour batter into prepared cake tin and bake at 170 °C for 50 minutes-1 hour, on middle shelf of oven. Leave cake in tin for 10 minutes, then turn out onto a wire rack to cool. Sprinkle with icing sugar or castor sugar for decoration. Makes 1 cake.

Coconut triem: Use 100 g desiccated coconut instead of glacé cherries tossed in flour.

CINNAMON CARROT CAKE

A popular modern recipe with a cream cheese topping.

250 ml brown sugar
250 ml sunflower oil
3 large eggs, beaten
10 ml ground cinnamon
5 ml bicarbonate of soda
375 ml self-raising flour
7 ml baking powder
350 ml finely grated carrots
250 ml chopped walnuts

Topping
250 ml cream cheese
5 ml vanilla essence
25 ml castor sugar

Mix sugar and oil and stir in beaten eggs. Add cinnamon and bicarbonate of soda. Stir, then add sifted flour, baking powder, carrots and walnuts. Pour into a large deep square cake tin and bake at 180 °C for 35-45 minutes, or until a skewer inserted in centre comes out clean. Cool in tin for 10 minutes, then turn out onto a wire rack to cool completely. *Topping:* Combine all ingredients well and spoon over top of cooled cake. Makes 1 large cake.

KLOP EN GEBAK

A delicious square cake topped with strawberry jam and whipped cream. Its name probably comes from the way the eggs and sugar are beaten until creamy. It is a very economical and versatile cake.

4 large eggs
500 ml castor sugar
250 ml sunflower oil
10 ml vanilla essence
500 ml cake flour
20 ml baking powder
300 ml milk

Mix eggs and castor sugar until creamy and sugar has dissolved. Add oil and vanilla essence and mix thoroughly. Add sifted flour and baking powder and stir to mix. Add enough milk to make a fairly slack mixture. Spoon batter into a large well-greased and lined square or rectangular cake tin and bake at 180 °C for 30 minutes, or until well-risen and lightly golden. Spread strawberry jam over cake and top with whipped fresh cream. Makes 1 cake.

Variations
• Cut cake into squares and decorate with whipped fresh cream, chocolate, nuts or cherries.
• Spread smooth apricot jam over cake and sprinkle with desiccated coconut before cutting into squares.
• Leave out milk and add 200 ml boiling water and 50 ml cocoa powder.

Note
• This mixture is enough for a large cake. Quantities can be halved for a smaller cake, and the baking time should then be decreased to 20 minutes.

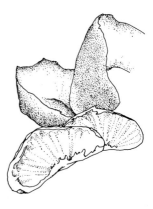

'Klop en gebak', a square cake sometimes cut into smaller shapes and colourfully decorated.

SNOWBALLS

These small cakes are dipped in jam and rolled in coconut.

150 g butter or margarine
250 ml castor sugar
3 eggs
500 ml self-raising flour
5 ml baking powder
150 ml fresh orange juice
5 ml finely grated orange rind

Decoration
250 ml smooth jam of your choice
125 ml water
150 g desiccated coconut

Cream butter or margarine and sugar until light and fluffy. Add eggs one at a time, beating well after each addition. Sift flour amd baking powder into a bowl. Fold flour into creamed mixture alternately with orange juice and rind and mix well to form a smooth batter. Grease patty pan tins well and fill hollows two thirds full with batter. Bake at 190 °C for 15 minutes, or until golden brown. Leave cakes to cool slightly in tins then turn out onto wire racks to cool completely. *Decoration:* Simmer jam and water in a saucepan over low heat until jam has melted, about 5 minutes, stirring often. Place coconut in a paper or plastic bag. Using a slotted spoon, dip each cake in jam sauce, coating well. Drain and shake in coconut to coat well. Makes 24.

JOHNSON'S SPECIALS

Little squares of vanilla cake, dipped in chocolate sauce then rolled in coconut.

4 large eggs
500 ml castor sugar
250 ml sunflower oil
10 ml vanilla essence
625 ml cake flour
15 ml baking powder
250 ml milk

Coating
500 ml icing sugar
60 ml cocoa powder
60 ml softened butter or margarine
200 ml hot water
200 ml desiccated coconut

From top to bottom: *Johnson's specials and Snowballs.*

Beat eggs and castor sugar until sugar has dissolved. Add oil and vanilla essence and mix well. Add sifted flour and baking powder and stir to combine. Stir in milk to make a smooth dropping consistency. Spoon into a greased and lined deep 40 x 30 cm baking tin and bake at 180 °C for 30 minutes. Allow to cool in tin for 10 minutes before turning out onto a wire rack to cool. Cut into small squares and set aside. *Coating:* Mix icing sugar, cocoa and butter or margarine to a paste, adding enough water to make a thin coating sauce. Using a slotted spoon, dip each cake square in the sauce, then roll in coconut and place in paper cases. Allow to set. Makes 50.

Variations
• Pipe fresh whipped cream on top of chocolate instead of rolling in coconut and decorate with grated chocolate.
• Pipe caramelised condensed milk on top of chocolate instead of rolling in coconut, and decorate with walnut halves.

HERTZOGGIES

These traditional Malay cookies are pastry cases baked with coconut meringue on one side. Apple jelly is then spooned over the other side when the hertzoggies have cooled.

250 g butter or margarine
60 ml sunflower oil
200 ml sugar
2 egg yolks
10 ml lemon essence
2 ml ground dried naartjie peel
500 ml self-raising flour
500 ml cake flour
pinch salt

Filling
2 egg whites
150 ml sugar
300 ml desiccated coconut
300 ml apple jelly or apricot jam

Cream butter, oil and sugar until light and creamy. Add egg yolks one at a time, beating well after each addition. Stir in lemon essence and naartjie peel. Sift flours and salt and mix into creamed mixture to make a very soft dough. Roll out to 6 mm thick on a lightly floured surface and cut out rounds with a fluted biscuit cutter. Place rounds in greased patty pans. *Filling:* Beat egg whites stiffly, adding sugar gradually. Stir in coconut, mixing well. Place 5 ml mixture on half of each pastry round and bake at 180 °C for 12-15 minutes. Remove from pans and cool on a wire rack. When cool, spoon 5 ml apple jelly or apricot jam onto rounds, next to coconut filling. Makes 60.

PUFF PASTRY

1 kg cake flour
15 ml cream of tartar
250 ml cornflour
2 extra large egg yolks
10 ml white vinegar
5 ml salt
10 ml sugar
200 g margarine
500 ml iced water
750 g cold butter

Sift 250 ml cake flour and 10 ml cream of tartar into a bowl and set aside. Sift 250 ml cornflour and 5 ml cream of tartar into a bowl and set aside. Beat egg yolks and vinegar and set aside. Sift remaining flour with salt and sugar into a mixing bowl and rub in margarine until mixture resembles coarse breadcrumbs. Add iced water to egg mixture and mix well. Add gradually to flour, working very lightly to form a soft, smooth and elastic dough. Sprinkle some of the cornflour mixture over and roll dough out to a rectangle on a lightly floured surface. Sprinkle with cornflour mixture and allow to rest for 15 minutes. Divide butter into 4 portions. Grate 1 portion over two thirds of dough and sprinkle cornflour mixture over. Fold a third of the dough over, sprinkling top with cornflour mixture, then fold over other third like an envelope. Set aside to rest for at least 30 minutes. Repeat 3 times, until butter has all been used, sprinkling with reserved flour mixture. Wrap dough in foil or waxproof paper and refrigerate for 12 hours before use. Makes 2 kg

Cook's tip
When making pastry remember:
• Keep utensils and ingredients as cold as possible.
• Roll out lightly and evenly; don't press dough with the rolling pin.
• Do not pull or stretch dough while rolling out.
• Do not handle dough too much.

JELLY FANCIES

These are the baked hertzoggie shells filled with a colourful array of well set jellies. Serve with cream piped round the edge at weddings and other special occasions.

250 g butter or margarine
60 ml sunflower oil
200 ml sugar
2 egg yolks
10 ml lemon essence
500 ml self-raising flour
500 ml cake flour
pinch salt

Filling
1 x 80 g packet red jelly
1 x 80 g packet green jelly
500 ml boiling water
300 ml iced water
125 ml cream

Cream butter, oil and sugar until light and fluffy. Add egg yolks, one at a time, beating well after each addition. Stir in lemon essence. Sift flours and salt and mix into creamed mixture to make a very soft dough. Roll out to 6 mm thick on a lightly floured surface and cut out rounds with a fluted biscuit cutter. Place rounds in greased patty pans, prick with a fork and bake blind for 10-12 minutes, or until golden brown. Turn out onto wire racks to cool. *Filling:* Mix each packet of jelly separately with 250 ml boiling water and 150 ml iced water. Allow to set. Whip cream until stiff. Scoop 5 ml of each colour of jelly into each pastry case and pipe cream around edge. Makes 50.

Variation
• Instead of jelly filling, slice 2 bananas and arrange slices in cases. Top with canned caramelised condensed milk topping and pipe whipped cream around edge.

Cook's tip
• Baked pastry cases may be frozen, interleaved with plastic, until needed.

PASTRY COPENHAGENS

Easily made using packaged pastry.

500 g flaky pastry
125 ml seedless raisins
brown sugar
1 egg, beaten
250 ml icing sugar
30 ml water

Roll pastry out thinly on a lightly floured surface and cut out 24 squares, each 10 x 10 cm. Sprinkle each square with about 5 ml raisins and brown sugar to taste. Roll each very thinly into a rope and wind in a concentric circle, tucking end underneath. Place on ungreased baking sheets and brush with beaten egg. Bake at 230 °C for 5 minutes, then reduce temperature to 200 °C and bake a further 8-10 minutes, or until lightly browned. Remove from baking sheets and cool on wire racks. Mix icing sugar and water and drizzle over copenhagens. Makes 24.

From top to bottom: *Caramel and banana fancies, traditional Malay hertzoggies, Jelly fancies and another way of presenting Caramel fancies.*

From left to right: ***Raisin tartlets, Apple tartlets, Klappertertjies, and Jam tartlets.***

JAM TARTLETS

These pastry cases freeze well and can be filled at the last minute. This recipe can also be used to bake one large tart.

500 g puff pastry* or flaky pastry
1 egg, beaten
250 ml apricot jam

Roll dough out to 3 mm thick and cut out 100 rounds 6 cm in diameter with a biscuit cutter. Cut a 1 cm diameter hole in 50 rounds. Moisten whole rounds with water and place a round with a hole in it on top of each. Place on ungreased baking sheets and brush with beaten egg. Bake at 230 °C for 4 minutes. Reduce heat to 200 °C and bake a further 5 minutes, or until lightly golden. Remove from baking sheets and cool on wire racks. Spoon 5 ml apricot jam in each pastry case. Makes 50.

Klappertertjies: Spoon 10 ml coconut filling into pastry cases instead of jam. Use coconut topping recipe given for Koesisters*.

Coconut almond tartlets: Add about 50 g blanched chopped almonds to coconut topping recipe given for Koesisters* and spoon into pastry cases instead of jam.

RAISIN TARTS

A typically Malay recipe, rich and fruity. It can also be served with cream or custard for dessert.

500 g puff pastry* or flaky pastry
beaten egg

Filling
250 ml seedless raisins
250 ml sultanas
60 ml water
30 ml sugar
20 ml butter
2 ml ground cinnamon

Divide pastry dough in 2 and roll each out to a round 20 cm in diameter. Use to line 2 pie dishes, cutting off and reserving excess. *Filling:* Boil raisins and sultanas in water until plump, about 5 minutes. Add sugar, butter and cinnamon and cook until nearly dry. Filling should not be watery. Set aside to cool, then spread in pie dishes. Roll out leftover dough, cut into strips and arrange in a lattice pattern over filling. Brush with beaten egg and bake at 230 °C for 10 minutes, then reduce heat to 200 °C and bake a further 10 minutes. Makes 2 tarts.

APPLE TARTLETS

500 g puff pastry*
1 egg, beaten
castor sugar

Filling
20 ml butter
1 kg cooking apples, peeled, cored and thinly sliced
50 ml sultanas
100 ml seedless raisins
75 ml brown sugar
grated rind of 1 lemon

Roll pastry out into a large square and cut out 24 squares, each 10 x 10 cm. *Filling:* Melt butter in a saucepan, add apples, sultanas, raisins, sugar and lemon rind and cook, covered, for 10 minutes, stirring often to prevent sticking. Set aside to cool. Place 15 ml apple filling on 1 triangle half of each square and fold other half over to make a triangle. Dampen edges with water and press together to seal. Place on ungreased baking sheets, brush lightly with beaten egg and bake for 10 minutes at 200 °C. Reduce temperature to 180 °C and bake for 15 minutes. Remove from oven, sprinkle with castor sugar and serve. Alternatively, drizzle with glacé icing made by combining 250 ml icing sugar and 30 ml water. Makes 24.

Religious Festivals and Ceremonies

Cape Malays adhere strictly to Islamic religious customs on feast days and holy days so that we find certain foods are served on special occasions.

Ramadan
Of all Muslim fasts this is the most important. During this month, the 9th month of the Islamic calendar, food and drink is prohibited from sunrise to sunset. Once night falls, however, the fast is usually broken with some dates, water, koesisters, pancakes or vetkoekies. Thereafter soup is served and sometimes boeber, a thick milky drink, which is always served on the 15th night, celebrating the middle of Ramadan. After these light refreshments, prayers are held. This is followed by supper which can be anything from roast chicken to bredie or breyani or whatever takes the cook's fancy.

Before sunrise there is time for a light meal of cereal, porridge, toast, eggs and coffee. Again some people even prefer something heavier like steak and sausage.

Throughout the month of Ramadan, children will be seen carrying little plates of koesisters, pancakes and vetkoekies to their neighbours before sundown. In a neighbourhood with a large Muslim community, as many as a dozen different kinds of cake can be seen on the tables every night.

Eidul-fitr (Labarang Ramadan)
The Festival of Charity or *Eidul-fitr* is celebrated on the night following the conclusion of Ramadan and it is traditional on this day to greet any Muslim with 'Eid Mubarak' or 'Slamat' meaning 'Happy Eid'. This is the most festive of occasions, when charity (fitra) is given to the poor by those Muslim households who can afford it, after which celebrations are held. The night before, special attention and care is taken in preparing foods for Eid lunch. More expensive dishes like crayfish curry, breyani, trifle and glacé fruit cake are reserved for this day. The afternoon would normally be spent visiting family and friends.

Eidul-Adha (Labarang Hadj)
The Feast of Sacrifice of *Eidul-Adha* is usually celebrated about 70 days after

Ramadan. This takes place the day after the pilgrims come back from Mount Arafah (*Jabal Ragmah*) where they beg the Almighty for forgiveness. A young goat or lamb is sacrificed at least once in the life of a Muslim, but more often if he can afford it. A third of the meat is distributed to the needy, while the remainder is shared between family and friends.

Rampisny (Moulidun-n-nabi)
The feast of the Orange Leaves marks the Prophet's birthday. Women, dressed in their beautiful satin finery, make their way to the Mosque with a knife and cutting board to shred piles of orange or lemon leaves. These are mixed with fragrant oils and tucked into small sachets made of colourful squares of folded tissue paper. The sachets are presented to the men attending the Mosque in the evening. During the afternoon, tea is served and the ladies sample a colourful assortment of cakes, biscuits, melktert and klappertert, as well as a variety of homemade preserves.

Engagements
It is still traditional for the future bridegroom's parents to request the bride-to-be's parents for her hand in marriage and between them they will set a date for the wedding. The bridegroom's family normally come bearing gifts of watches, an engagement ring, flowers, bowls of fruit wrapped in cellophane and ribbon, chocolates and perfume. In return they will receive cut-glass bowls of cake and other fancy foods.

Weddings
Of all the Malay feasts, weddings are still the most elaborate. Usually two receptions are held, one for the groom and one for the bride. The reception could take the form of a tea, where fancy cakes, fresh fruits and preserves are served or it could be a more substantial lunch or supper. During the wedding ceremony the bride is represented by her father at the Mosque, while she remains at home. Traditionally the bride is sent a 'bride's basket' for her lunch or supper by her husband. This comprises carefully prepared dishes of food wrapped in

cellophane with pretty bows, an arrangement of flowers and a basket of fruit. Nowadays, however, the young couple may choose to forego this expensive custom.

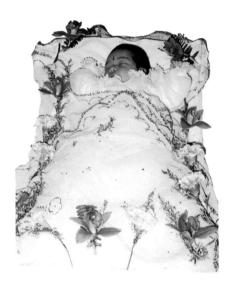

Doopmaal
Naming of the baby usually takes place on the 7th day after the birth. The baby is enshrouded in a *medoura*, a scarf embroidered with gold thread and decorated with flowers such as orchids, carnations and rosebuds. Relatives, friends and the Imam attend the ceremony, during which a lock of the baby's hair is cut off and something sweet, like a date, sugar or honey, is placed on the baby's lips while prayers are offered. Afterwards tea is served and is almost always accompanied by melktert.

Funerals (Janazah)
It is traditional for Muslim men to attend the funeral service in the Mosque and accompany the bier to the cemetery, while the women gather at the home of the deceased. After the men return, the mourners are usually provided with something to eat. In the past, this would have been wortel en ertjie bredie or sugar beans bredie, but nowadays mutton curry served with rice, sambals and salad, has taken preference as it is easier to prepare.

INDEX